SIN,
LIBERTY
and LAW

SIN, LIBERTY and LAW

by LOUIS MONDEN, S.J.

translated by Joseph Donceel, s.j.

SHEED AND WARD : NEW YORK

Originally published in Dutch under the title
VERNIEUWD GEWETEN, Descleé de Brouwer,
Bruges, Belgium. The French edition by the
same publisher appeared under the title LE
SENSE DU PECHE CHEZ L'HOMME MODERNE in
the series "La Bibliotheque d'Etudes Psycho-
Religieuse."

Nihil Obstat:
>   Thomas J. Beary
>   Censor Librorum

Imprimatur:
>   ✠ Robert F. Joyce
>   Bishop of Burlington
>   May 28, 1965

*The Nihil Obstat and Imprimatur are official dec-
larations that a book or pamphlet is free of doctrinal
or moral error. No implication is contained therein
that those who have granted the Nihil Obstat and
Imprimatur agree with the contents, opinions or
statements expressed.*

Library of Congress Catalog Card Number 65–20857

Manufactured in the United States of America

Contents

Contents

Introduction

Until quite lately there has been a widespread feeling among
Christians that they were witnessing the disappearance of all
awareness of sin and a frightening return to the law of the
jungle, an impression confirmed by the disorder of the first
post-war years. In such a climate Pius XII spoke his famous
words: "The greatest sin of our time is that it is losing the
very concept of sin." But meanwhile it has become evident
that, if in some domains there is a real blunting of the moral
sense, in others—e.g. that of social justice, of tolerance, of
unselfish concern for the underprivileged portions of mankind
—this moral sense has grown remarkably stronger and deeper.
Obviously the sense of sin has not vanished but has simply
undergone a considerable change. Possibly that change, a
factor in the mutation which is taking place in our whole
conception of the world and of man, is not a phenomenon of
decay but of maturation, one aspect of man's growing towards
a new adulthood.

The ramifications of my theme cover the whole field of
theology. I have tried to confine myself to the specific problem of the evolving sense of sin at the risk of disappointing
readers seeking answers to related problems. The temptation
was especially strong, when I was trying to project the pro-

posed solutions onto the pastoral plane, to make detailed
applications to specific problems of moral theology which are
real and very much at issue. But this would have led me
beyond the aim and scope of the present work. I have tried
to resist that temptation, and the reader will find no more
than a few allusions to such problems.

In order to make the book accessible not only to priests,
but also to all cultivated laymen, I have avoided as far as
possible all technical terminology and endeavored to keep
the study of the questions under investigation within reason-
able limits. The rather extensive bibliography presented in
the notes is likewise compiled more for the priest in the parish
and for the layman than for the specialist.[1]

SIN,
LIBERTY
and LAW

1

The Meaning of the Words

In recent years the question of theological language has become one of the main problems—perhaps *the* main problem—of theological methodology. First, much attention is given to the search for the most appropriate categories into which to translate God's message. Theologians weigh the advantages and disadvantages of a less technical terminology, one not bound to certain philosophical schools; likewise of a wider use of images and concepts belonging to the Bible. Next there is felt a growing need, whatever the terminology used, to determine precisely the logical status of these terms, clearly to distinguish their several *levels of signification* and to define exactly the linguistic field within which they can meaningfully be used.

There is no domain of thought where such work is more indispensable than that of Christian moral theology. For until recently the practice prevailed of treating concepts such as guilt, sin, duty, contrition, conscience as if they were univocal terms, endowed with a clearly defined, unchangeable meaning. Most of our contemporaries continue to do so, and even in present-day theological publications this vague and confusing use of language is frequent. Yet philosophical analysis, especially phenomenology and linguistic philosophy, using the discoveries of psychology and sociology, has reached the conclusion that each one of these terms covers many and quite different meanings, irreducible to each other, which should be clearly distinguished if one is not to introduce insidious ambiguities into theological discussion, with the danger that there will be no real meeting of minds, since the same words are employed on totally different levels of signification and within quite different domains of application.

THE THREE LEVELS OF ETHICS

We might use the word "ethics"—somewhat arbitrarily, to be sure, but we cannot do without some well-defined terminology—for the whole of man's modes of being and of behaving in their undivided totality. The ethical conduct of man may then be considered on *three fundamental levels,* whereby the selfsame terms of the ethical vocabulary receive a wholly different meaning.[2]

THE LEVEL OF INSTINCT

When an animal's drive fails to reach its goal, because of the resistance of things or the competition of another animal or a human sanction, that drive may give rise to behavior which—especially in domesticated animals, whose reflexes are heavily conditioned by human contact—strongly resembles the conduct of a human being who feels or is guilty. In man too there is an experience of guilt and a sense of duty which, although strongly influenced by the intellect and rationalized with higher motives, stands essentially upon *the level of instinct.*

The *law* which directs this instinctive ethics comes not from within but from without, from the pressure of reality, and especially of society, which, by means of prohibitions and "taboos," builds a dam against the impulses of individual instinctivity. Although this pressure is introjected by the individual and turns into instinctive self-control, into a feeling of *obligation,* that "ought" is always felt as something alien to the person, even as something hostile to his instinctive impulses. Hence it is experienced with an ambivalence of rebellious resistance, neutralized by fear of sanctions or of failure and by the impression that the pressure is irresistible. That ambivalent feeling, which is not experienced as lucid insight but undergone as an instinctive warning, is, on this level, called *conscience.*

Guilt and *sin* of this kind consist in the material transgression of some prohibition or taboo. Whether the intention was good or not, the purpose wrong or nonexistent, the action performed freely or without freedom—all this has no bearing on guilt. The sin consists in the material fact of "transgression"; this or that action, this or that object, is *ipso facto* sinful. The ensuing reaction is equally instinctive, although it may be rationalized with all kinds of moral considerations. It is a blind *feeling,* rather than a consciousness *of guilt;* it derives from the awareness not of having acted badly, irrationally, against one's conscience, but of having acted wrongly, faultily, against some order. It is an almost physical occult sense that one has strayed beyond a safe boundary and is now threatened with the vengeance of the mysterious power that guards it; a feeling of anxiety which makes one cower instinctively in expectation of the coming punishment and experience something almost like relief when it finally does come.

Contrition for sin too is, on this level, not an awareness of one's wickedness and a desire for amendment, i.e. for becoming one's good self again, but simply the instinctive urge to escape the consequences of the transgression. On this level contrition looks mostly for formulas, rites of reconciliation and magic gestures by means of which the angered powers may be placated, the transgression undone, the punishment avoided and the safety of legal limits regained. *Confession* of the fault, expression of a *firm resolve* to stay henceforth within the limits of the law, all this belongs to the conjuring rites. Both are sincerely meant, not however in the sense of a personal decision, but as an instinctive anxiety reflex: "I'll never dare do such a thing again, too bad I ever ran that risk."

THE MORAL LEVEL

We shall use the word "moral" here not in the general meaning of ethical conduct, but in the specific sense of the element in this ethical conduct which belongs to the level of the conscious and free self-realization of the human person. Hence "moral" refers to the most human aspect of the ethical. It is present where man, having reached adult conscious insight, fully realizes the conditions of his free and authentic self-development as a spirit in the world, in communion with his fellow men and in union with the absolute Spirit, God.

On this level the *law* is no longer a pressure from without. It is based ultimately on man's essential dependence on God. In practice it is experienced as autonomous, with an autonomy that does not reject every kind of dependence but emphasizes the fact that even man's profound dependence on God can manifest itself only through the structure and the growth of his own nature as a source of moral obligation. What man experiences as law is nothing but his own essential growth as a proffered possibility and as a task to be fulfilled; it is the direction towards total self-development which corresponds most closely to the structure of the inner self, put before the free act as an absolute demand. This absolute demand is moral *obligation*: man's freedom owes it to itself to be faithful to its authentic self-development. And *conscience* is the deepest self-consciousness of man, insofar as it acts as a power of discrimination deciding in every choice what will promote authentic self-realization and what will stand in its way. That conscience is not infallible, because it depends on the information it receives about a moral problem in a definite situation; hence it can err in good faith owing to insufficient data or the incorrect judgment of some situation. Yet the voice of conscience, even when erring in good faith, must unconditionally be obeyed.

There is moral *guilt* where the free will acts against conscience. It never consists in the matter of the action taken objectively. Only the free choice and the wrong direction taken by the will must be considered. Moral guilt is always freely chosen infidelity to authentic self-realization and the free yielding to a pseudo-value. The objectively wrong action which conscience considers good is not morally guilty. The objectively good action which conscience, in good faith, deems wrong is morally guilty. Likewise *punishment* for such an action is no longer feared from without, as the vengeance of a mysterious offended power. The guilty deed punishes itself, because it is a self-inflicted wound, a matter of growing in the wrong direction. Considered from without, the sinful course may look like the free unfolding of life and of one's own sovereign vitality; in fact it always means a denying of oneself, the teeming within one's soul of spiritual weeds or cancerous growths.

Hence on the level of morality *contrition* will always be the inner acknowledgement of an action as self-negation, the uttering of a verdict of guilty over one's own deviations, not as a resigned recording of some failure but as an active will to correct the deviation and as a steady *resolve* to restore and to make up for the missed occasions of self-development by a more vigorous moral growth in the future. The *confession* of one's guilt adds nothing to the value of the inner self-judgment. It may be one of the many means used for recovery, because it places one's self-condemnation and steady resolve in the concrete framework of one's moral development within a human community.

THE CHRISTIAN-RELIGIOUS LEVEL

The moral self-unfolding of man mentioned in the previous paragraph takes place mainly through the development of his personality in an adult, loving self-donation to others. On the moral level, however, ethical conduct does not find its norms directly in this self-donation, but in the degree of authenticity of human self-realization as expressed in that self-donation. Hence when that natural self-unfolding is raised to a totally new level of value, as it is gratuitously assumed into a divine intimacy of love, this intimacy itself must become the only norm of the new ethical conduct of the human partner in his dialog with God.

The *law* which guides this meeting with God is no longer the growth of one's own being, but the proffered invitation to rise above that level towards a new meeting in love, an invitation which is at once possibility, question, offer, and, in its own way, exigency for total donation. At first it looks as if the autonomy of self-decision has been given up once more for a law forced upon man from without. In fact there is no coercion from without, no giving up of one's own self-development, but a yielding in love to a God who is *intimior intimo meo* ("closer to me than I am to myself"), so that letting oneself go in this love entails a higher and deeper self-realization, a real divinization of man.

Whereas the outer pressure of taboo upon instinct entailed

an inframoral heteronomy of the law, the heteronomy of the divine invitation to love is the basis of a supramoral ethics. This is true also of the *obligation* imposed by that law: moral duty is not suppressed by it, but assumed in a totally new "ought" which is even further removed from all coercion than moral obligation and might be called a "vocation" rather than an "obligation." The specific forms of this "ought" considerably transcend the moral forms; they lie in the domain of what might be designated as "counsel" or "beatitude." *Conscience* on this level will be love itself as a power of discriminating what can promote from what will hinder its growth. It is no longer a natural or rational insight—although moral insight continues to act in the religious conscience—but an affinity with the beloved, a communion in feeling and in thinking, a "connaturality" with him.

Here *guilt* and *sin* are less than ever a material action, nor are they even the impairing of one's own power of growth. They consist in saying No to love. Sin becomes man himself in a relation of refusal to God's love. Hence, on this religious level, a merely material transgression can never be a sin. A moral fault can, but owing to the religious relation it acquires a new dimension, because refusing to be oneself turns into refusing to be for the Other. Over and above the moral fault there is a specific religious refusal, a violation of divine love in itself, a kind of guilt which is now in the fullest meaning of that word a "sin." The *punishment* for that sin, too, is not a threat impending from without but the enduring invitation of love itself as the torment of him who rejects it.

On this level *contrition* too becomes a function of love: it is the awareness of our unfaithfulness to love, joined to our conviction that this love surpasses every infidelity, that "God is greater than our heart." Religious contrition is therefore infinitely more than a search for security from the avenging

wrath of an offended power; much more, too, than self-condemnation and a will for restoration. It is an appeal to the
mercy of the beloved, a certitude that love will accept the
guilt which we confidently offer and turn it into a new increase of the love relationship. It is our boldness in converting
the fault into a trustful offering of love. The answer to this
contrition—for on this level of the meeting of persons a response always comes—is *forgiveness*. A word devoid of meaning on the instinctive and the ethical levels, on the religious
level it means the creative restoration of love through the
integration of the fault within its growth. It is not a gradual
reparation which remedies the fault, but the resumption of
the love relationship, the reawakening of love itself, out of the
meeting of mercy and repentance. And precisely because this
meeting is granted by God in a fully gratuitous manner, love
can be restored more wonderfully than ever in one creative
moment of mercy. The *confession* of the fault is the sign,
the opening word of the dialog in which the encounter takes
place. And penance or *reparation* is the making real, on the
level of moral growth, of what has already become a reality
on the religious level in the one creative moment of love.

The distinction between the three levels of the ethical might
become clearer from a consideration of how one and the same
concrete situation can be experienced on each of them.

A young mother has given birth to a deformed baby. All
her instinctive love and possessiveness surges in rebellion.
Instinct says: "It is better not to let this child live. It can
grow up only for a life which will be a hell, it will not know
one moment of happiness." "Happiness" is understood here
on the instinctive level as health, beauty, success, acceptance,
the possibility of realizing one's plans. Underneath the instinctive compassion for the child the voice of self-pity too may
be heard: fear of all the selfless love which such a child will

demand, of the innumerable humiliations which may be expected. Against the impulse of instinct the only barrier is the law: it is forbidden, I may not do it, they don't allow this, I will be punished for doing it. If, at a given moment, the pressure of instinct prevails and the action is performed against the pressure of external law, then everything will depend on the reaction of society. If the courts and public opinion are in the main hostile, the young mother breaks down under her feeling of guilt. On the other hand, should public opinion show itself favorably disposed (and public opinion too will almost unavoidably move on the level of instinct in its judgment about love and happiness) and force the law to approve —or, at least, to acquit—then all feeling of guilt is gone. The brakes are off; "Now it is allowed." One is even proud of having had the courage to force the external law to open this gate, of having breached the wall of social pressure by the sheer force of the maternal drive. In all this there is not the slightest element of moral judgment.

It is quite a different matter if the mother wishes to make her decision on the *moral level*. In that case, independently of any concern for legislation or eventual consequences, she will ask herself: "Have I a right to interfere with this life which has been entrusted to me? I am responsible for the meaning which this young life will one day possess. Have I ever any right to say that a human life has no meaning?" Her idea of human happiness, too, will no longer be merely instinctive, corresponding to the public norms of wealth, success and social acceptance. She will have to ask, "What are the ingredients of real happiness? How can we explain the fact that people who seem to have none of the things instinct considers essential for happiness call themselves happy, and others who seem to have all these things in abundance commit suicide? Might not the meaning of human life depend mainly on the meaning one gives to it—on the meaning which, from the start, the love of the parents bestows on it? Is the action instinct is trying to force on me a real gesture of mercy, or is it an attempt against what is authentically human? Only the answer to this last question can be decisive, and if the young mother goes against it she will keep on feeling guilty even if all the courts acquit her and public opinion hails her as a heroine.

Finally, the young mother who is a Christian, who from the very start puts herself on the *religious level*, will not even have to deliberate. From the beginning of her pregnancy she has felt that the new life growing within her was a mandate and an invitation of God's love. Neither wealth nor success nor complete self-fulfillment is for her the meaning of human existence or the norm of happiness. To her every life means an invitation to grow in loving intimacy with God, and every human being, in the shelter of that depth of love, can find the strength to fulfill his own task and vocation in love and happiness. She knows that as a mother she is called to love that child too, with all her resources for sacrifice and suffering, in such a way that she may teach him to accept his painful yet beautiful destiny, and make him capable of authentic love and real human and divine happiness. For her the rejection of that mandate, however burdensome and difficult it may look, would be to reject God's invitation, to doubt the love which beckons and run away from the suffering involved in the task which is set before her.

MUTUAL RELATION OF THESE THREE LEVELS

For the sake of clarity we have made a very sharp distinction between the three levels of signification of the ethical vocabulary. This does not, however, mean that they are hermetically sealed off from each other. All three are forms of human experience, and no one of them is ever totally free of resonances and influences emanating from the other two. Man's psychological life is never exclusively spiritual or exclusively instinctual. The religious element is never independent of intellect or instinct. The lower level will always be implicitly present and active in the higher. The higher level will always rest on all the lower levels as a substratum, assuming them into itself and imparting a new and higher meaning to them. The growth of human psychic life will always proceed from instinct to spiritual self-development and culminate in religious self-donation. This is true not only of every individual but also of the moral development of humanity as a whole.

In *individual existence* the child appears at first as a bundle of instincts seeking gratification. The clash of these instincts with a refractory reality, especially their meeting with a partly acquiescing, partly restricting, directing, punishing attitude on the part of the parents, evokes in the child the first feelings of duty and of guilt, still entirely on the level of taboo. This does not mean that the child as yet possesses no spiritual experience, but that the spiritual element is still no more than implicit, manifesting itself only in projections within instinctive activities. Even when, around the age of four, external parental authority is introjected within the psyche of the child himself, becoming thus, as it were, an endopsychic counterpart of instinct, that "superego," as depth psychology calls it, is not yet a spiritual consciousness, directing in full clarity the impulses of instinct towards human self-realization. It remains a collection of taboo commands and taboo prohibitions, which is only gradually taken over by a developing consciousness and transformed into a personal "conscience."

The "age of reason," which traditional moral doctrine places around seven years, appears in this respect to be a very arbitrary boundary line, although we must grant that the first flashes of spiritual self-possession do indeed occur around that time. They enable the child to put some conscious order into the domain of his instincts, at least if the problems encountered remain within the dimensions of the child's own world.

The growth towards maturity will depend precisely on the gradual self-conquest of consciousness and on the capacity for integrating the instinctive impulses ever more harmoniously within that conscious self-development. We do not mean that man gradually breaks away from his instinctivity into undiluted spirituality. Such "angelism" fails to take into account the unity of the human body-soul composite. Man continues to carry within him not only his instinctivity but also his whole past, with all the experiences, reflexes and habitual automatisms, with all the feelings of guilt and anxiety and coercion which the child has experienced within the world of taboo.

We may try to picture the development towards ideal moral maturity in a hypothetical case: that of a child in whom the world of taboo morality is a perfect prefiguration, within infantile dimensions, of the moral norm of life which conscious self-development will later propose as an ideal. There would be a real analogy between the child's morality and that of the adult: the growing self-consciousness would consist in a gradual and harmonious personalization, not so much of the impersonal as of the prepersonal infantile elements. The habits, reflexes and automatisms, in such a hypothetical case, constitute a safe, harmonious, instinctive substructure for the morality of the adult. There would be no discordance between the warning signal of instinctive feelings of duty or guilt arising from the unconscious past and the consciously recognized duty or guilt. It is obvious that the superego will not have this prefigurative harmony in everybody and that in cases where early education has had a less favorable outcome the integration of the superego within the conscious moral personality will take place much less smoothly. There is even some danger that the integration may be so much hampered that the adult never quite proceeds beyond the childish taboo conscience but bogs down in a morality which is for the most part instinctive, one which he will endeavor to rationalize with the full resources of his intellect and his culture.

The *religious reality* of God's grace can likewise be present in the baptized child from the very beginning as a new essential relation to God, not detached from the natural existence either of the spirit or of the instincts. The role of grace is to leaven and to raise this whole reality, "integrating" or harmoniously assuming it in its turn within the divine dialog. In this process divine grace itself will be influenced by the course of natural growth. In the small child the world of faith will take shape only within the child's world of images and under the form of projections. Religious conduct and religious feelings of guilt will long remain only implicit within the taboo morality of the superego. Even the seemingly adult religious ideology of asceticism, penance, self-donation and sacrifice may be alloyed by a number of infantile taboo elements. Furthermore, the religious relation may come into conflict with a too anthropomorphic ethic which is able to conceive the meeting with God only in terms of a personal conquest and in which a natural adult pride refuses a supernatural self-donation. When the religious relation enters a human life only in the adult years, as in a "conversion," the conflict with the residue of taboo morality and the purely natural ethical attitude of the past will be more acute and the slow integration of life within the sphere of grace will take place even more laboriously and more gradually.

Moral adulthood does not, therefore, simply coincide with bodily or even with spiritual adulthood. In a person adult in years, moral infantilism may accompany a high degree of intellectual development, cultural refinement, a deep psychological insight and a wealth of human experience. Moral adulthood, in its turn, does not necessarily go along with *religious-ethical adulthood*: a person who is highly developed morally may remain undeveloped religiously or may cling to infantile forms of religiosity.

Mankind likewise grows into adulthood. In mankind too there has probably been a very gradual growth from a largely implicit moral choice caught up in taboos to a clarified moral insight. The Christian awareness of sin as well has undergone a divine preparation, through the slow breaking away of the religious conscience from the taboo and magical implications in which it was at first confined—as shown in the Bible stories —until Christ, in the fullness of time, could propose the mature purity of this religious awareness of sin. It is the confluence of moral insight developed to adult lucidity in Greek thought with the religious conscience as fully revealed within the Christian religion which has given Western ethics its specific character. Even sociologically, the "guilt cultures" of the West (where the ethical norm consists in the self-experienced personal value) are often contrasted with the "shame cultures" of other places (in which the norm of ethical action consists in social acceptance).*

---

* See M. B. Singer, *Shame and Guilt* (Springfield, Ill., Thomas, 1953). Japanese morality, considered as a typical "morality based on shame," is very well described in R. Benedict's *The Chrysanthemum and the Sword* (Boston, Houghton, 1946). David Riesman, in *The Lonely Crowd* (New Haven, Yale, 1950), discovers a trend in this country towards an increasingly less "inner-directed" and a gradually more "outer-directed" morality.

Further development of these historical considerations is not within the scope of this book.

PRESENT-DAY PROBLEMS

An awareness of the complexity of our ethical activity presents modern moral theology with a number of problems, among which we would like to consider three in particular.

A *first series* of questions refers to the *relation between freedom and determinism* in the actual ethical activity of the average human being. Even if one does not deny human freedom in theory, the question arises as to what extent the average person in fact escapes mere taboo morality. Is not the pressure of biological heredity, of social influences, of unconscious inhibitions and complexes such that, for most people, the possibility of a real moral judgment is excluded? Furthermore, is it possible for a man to measure the real freedom in human actions—either in his own or in those of others—to isolate it in the network of determinisms in which they are, often unconsciously, caught? This involves all kinds of vexing practical problems—e.g., what is the real meaning of the notion of "mortal sin," and how does it remain possible to know what one must mention in confession as "mortal sin"? On the religious level the whole question arises of the relation between psychic health, maturity, and holiness.

A *second series* of questions refers to the relation between the inner spontaneity of *freedom* and the *law* imposed from without. Is there really a double morality, as taught by Bergson? Or does a reciprocal relation exist between them in which each is a prolongation of the other? Can the inner, spontaneous spiritual growth of man be formulated in a permanent, unchangeable natural law? Or is human nature an evolving structure developing historically in given situations, one which cannot be caught in rigid formulas, so that the individual moral judgment can, in the last analysis, be made only with reference to a concrete situation? Which shall we choose: an *ethics based on the natural law* or a *situational ethics*? And what is the relation between the religious law of love and the inner law of human growth and the external law imposed by society? Is it, as Hesnard claims, unavoidable that under the cloak of an evangelical law of love Christian ethics in fact always falls back to the level of an inframoral taboo ethics?

Finally, a *third series* of questions concerns the true relation between *moral effort* and *religious salvation* from evil. Do these two factors normally go together or are they to a large extent independent of each other? Is moral rectitude a help or rather a hindrance to the religious awareness of sin? Will one who is morally blameless unavoidably degenerate into a religious pharisee? And must we, then—in some kind of *"sin mystique"*—consider moral guilt as an almost indispensable condition for being received into grace and admitted to salvation?

The next three chapters are an effort to answer these three series of questions. Each time we shall try first to state the problem in as clear-cut and concrete a manner as possible; next we shall gather the data for a theoretical solution; finally we shall indicate a few orientations for a pastoral theology inspired by these principles.

2

Freedom and Determinism

A few years ago, during a symposium on morality and the art of the novel, a Catholic novelist said this to me: "I have a feeling that you priests harbor a double standard of sin, one for the pulpit and one for the confessional. When I hear you preaching on sin I shudder at all the evil alive in me. I kneel in the confessional full of sorrow, confess my sin and anxiously await the verdict. Lo and behold, I meet nothing but mildness and comprehension. The abstract wickedness of the pulpit has turned into a skein of concrete human actions in which a tiny bit of that wickedness is buried under an accumulation of human wretchedness, struggles and good intentions. We have before us no longer the frightening reality of 'the' sin, but the commonplace petty human reality of 'my' sin." And he added with a smile: "The trouble is that we try to write our novels in the confessional and you judge them from the pulpit."

This anecdote brings out rather well a primary point on which the mind of contemporary society refuses to accept the traditional notions of morality and sinfulness. Catholic moral teaching formulates its norms for the normal human being. But does that being exist? The Church's morality has as a basic presupposition that the majority of mankind reach moral and religious adulthood, and even the child, once he has come to the so-called age of reason, shares that adulthood sufficiently to be able, and obliged, to meet the requirements of the abstract norm. But is moral and religious adulthood, presupposed by that norm, not in fact a limit, an unreachable ideal, which finds only an analogous approximation and a timid beginning of realization in concrete mankind and in the concrete human being? Is the actual blending of freedom and determinism in man not such that he cannot discover the exact degree of his responsibility or evaluate reliably his own morality or sinfulness? And if this is true, what is the meaning of the confession of sins, of contrition and of the firm purpose of amendment, in and outside of the confessional? What norm can the spiritual director follow in guiding the conscience?

Let us first allow full expression to the objection. Afterwards we may try to establish the principles for a solution and, using them, make a few applications to the pastoral domain.

THE PROBLEM

Classic moral theology contains a treatise, *"de impedimentis libertatis"* (on the obstacles to freedom), which applies not only within moral doctrine but also within ecclesiastical legislation. It may even, to a great extent, have been transposed from jurisprudence to moral doctrine. A distinction is made between obstacles coming from within, mainly ignorance and the violence of instinctive impulses, and obstacles coming from without, mainly moral coercion, deceit and intimidation (*vis et metus*). In the light of the latest findings, however, these positions appear to be completely outmoded. They take for granted that man's freedom is a perfectly *autonomous power of decision,* hindered in the exercise of its sovereignty only accidentally, by factors which, although possibly often at work, remain by their nature exceptional. Quite different is the picture of man drawn by *contemporary anthropology.*

Here human freedom is seen as a freedom in situation, and the dialectic of freedom and determinism is considered essential for every human action. Only this dialectic makes freedom into really human freedom, and modern science seems to find it more difficult to preserve the moment of freedom than to point out all that is determined in man's activity.

The elements of determinism in man's activity can be traced back mainly to three sources—biological, social and psychological factors.[3]

BIOLOGICAL INFLUENCES

The data of biology concerning inherited handicaps, predisposition to certain deviations, hereditary transmission of temperament, of character with its qualities and its defects—all this has been known for a long time and has been acknowledged by traditional moral teaching, though often more in theory than in practice. Yet in this domain too the more recent discoveries of neuro-surgery (modifications of the personality brought about, e.g., by leucotomy or lobotomy), and of endocrinology (hormone treatments), the physiological interventions resulting in changes in the personality, the use of the famous "police drugs" and of truth serum, etc., have demonstrated, often spectacularly, not only to the scientific world but even to the general public, the influence—much greater than usually admitted—of the biological factors on the psyche, hence also on the freedom of moral action.

These exceptional interventions simply highlight the fact that man can at all times be influenced in such a manner. In the normal way this influence may be exercised by all kinds of other factors always at work in the environment, or arising from certain circumstances or artificially produced. Because of their effects, so closely resembling natural sleep, sleeping

pills, alcohol, opiates have been considered natural phenomena. The modern tranquilizers, on the other hand, which,
without any intoxicating effects, have the same pacifying effect
on man and his anxieties, have brought home much more
tellingly the profound influence which the physical environment can exert on the psyche, hence on freedom and on the
conscience. This is evidenced by the almost magical attraction
these drugs exert on most people.

The impression of determinism produced by all this is
strengthened by the inescapable evidence that the organism
of modern man, more specifically his nervous system, has not
yet been able to adapt itself to the rapidly changing conditions in the rhythms of human life, the tensions associated
with his work, his social responsibilities and the planetization
of existence. The mutation being experienced at the present
time by man and his world is submitting man to a painful
crisis of adaptation. His balance is much more unstable, his
vulnerability greater, his powers of resistance are often tested
to the extreme limit, and sometimes beyond endurance. From
Charlie Chaplin's *Modern Times* to *Mon Oncle* of Tati, from
Huxley's *Brave New World* through Georghiu's *Twenty-fifth
Hour* to Samuel Beckett's *Happy Days,* and from Huizinga's
Geschonden Wereld to *Le Petit Prince* of St. Exupéry, carica-
turists, novelists, essayists and cultural philosophers have called
attention to this threatening *robotization* of man by an over-
technical civilization. The same thing is brought out equally
well by the success of yoga and various methods of relaxation,
by the need for adaptations in such matters as the length of
working days, night rest, opportunities for recreation; by a
demand for greater flexibility in discipline and ascetical practices even within the Church and religious life. The very term
robotization points towards an increasing awareness of determinism, and the many concessions to weakened nervous sys-

tems contain an acknowledgment of the fact that the bodily condition may prevail over the most generous free will.

SOCIAL PRESSURE

Even less considered by traditional moral teaching, although it is equally or even more decisive than biological conditioning, is the influence of *social* factors, the pressure of society on the free activity of the individual. It is imperative that the classical notions of human respect, fear, shame, etc., should be given a broader and more far-reaching content than they have had until now.

Most human beings seem to be unable to think or to act with real autonomy; they are *mass products*, who feel, react and judge collectively, who are without defense against the pressure of prevailing opinions, propaganda slogans, the hidden persuaders of a clever advertising technique, the daily doses of suggestion served up as "objective" news releases by the opinion-shaping media of press, radio, movies and TV. Even so-called intellectuals are more susceptible to such influences than they like to think, especially since, to a great extent, these suggestions are received not on the level of clear consciousness but through the unconscious.

Even more powerful is the influence of the *affective relationships* in the narrower circle of the family or the environment in which one works or relaxes. An instinctive need, rarely emerging into consciousness, for safety, shelter, acceptance, esteem; competitiveness, aggressivity, doubts about oneself—all this often has a determining influence on the individual's attitudes and activity. The discoveries in the field of group psychology, group dynamics, group pedagogy and group therapy are, in this respect, both amazing and instructive. Sociological polls and sociographic inquiries confirm these data so thoroughly that one understands how some sociologists have systematized their conclusions into a philosophy which reduces moral conscience to a quasi-instinctive spiritual power of adaptation of the individual to the group within which he lives and on which his material, affective and spiritual existence depends. Even the untrained observer—enlightened by the widely disseminated discoveries of sociology—is having it borne in upon him that pressure groups and pressure factors are having enormous influence in all the domains of social life.

Thus, for example, it is clear to everyone that during a strike the freedom to work is restricted much more by the moral coercion of solidarity within the laboring class than by the material violence of pickets. Everyone sees with his own eyes how a person's freedom can be influenced by the color of his skin. It begins to dawn on us that what is called freedom of religion has no meaning if it involves the moral herding and isolating of the faithful in a spiritual ghetto. Every housewife experiences the decisive influence of public opinion in the matter of birth restriction, and recent trials have made it clear how difficult it is for a jury to resist the pressure of that same opinion.

Like the physical tensions, this social pressure has enormously *increased in our time* so that it becomes almost unbearable for the individual. The modern citizen is becoming more and more dependent on the red tape and intricate machinery of a complicated public administration in matters such as tax control, social security, urbanization, and so on. No longer is he able to reside, work, travel, advance in his profession, become ill, without interference. Everywhere he meets restrictions, licenses, diplomas, tests, files and certificates. It is not only his own society that holds him thus within its grip. He has the feeling that slowly the pressure of the whole world is beginning to weigh upon him. Constantly his way of life is depending more on the manner in which the whole planet is developing. A crisis in a small country he cannot even locate on the map brings about an acute outburst of hoarding in his own country, and a few cases of smallpox at the other side of the globe puts a whole continent in a state of panic. This increasing planetization of all relationships oppresses the individual with a crushing sense of his own helplessness, of being in the grip of powers which no force of personality can control.

Not only is man becoming more mechanized, he is also becoming gradually more socially *anonymous*, or depersonalized. Young people especially are acutely conscious of this restraint of freedom, and such social phenomena as the beatniks represent basically nothing more than sterile and impotent efforts to reassert personal freedom and creativeness in face of this irresistible pressure. All this is true for what is called, not without irony, the "free world." Of course it applies to a far greater extent to those countries where the social pressure apparatus is ruthlessly used by totalitarian powers to suppress every attempt at ideological opposition and crush all individual freedom. These countries are well aware that in the persecution of recusants, economic deprivation, the breaking of a career, herding into a ghetto, moral isolation through collective disapproval and boycott and the refined method of social and psychological pressure which has been called "brainwashing" offer better chances of success than the antiquated method of bloody purges and the making of martyrs.

INFLUENCE OF THE UNCONSCIOUS PAST

Yet the most decisive determinisms which lie in ambush against the freedom of human activity do not come from

without but are at work within the psyche itself, as a remnant
of man's own *past*. Classical moral theology knew the force
of habit, the way in which long-indulged passions enslave,
and the tragic manner in which we are overtaken by our own
actions. But it has taken depth psychology to reveal the true
dimensions of man's dependence on his own past and push
its boundaries back to the very first experiences of the child.
For, as we noted in the preceding chapter, man carries along
in his adult life all the experiences he underwent as a child,
when his moral bearings and his connection with God through
grace were still wholly implicit, first within the world of instinct, next within that of taboo morality and of the superego.
Like all first steps, these first experiences of the child are of
decisive importance for the further growth and orientation
of the person. But in the psychological realm the risks are far
greater, because the infant life with its imperfect consciousness and acute vulnerability is without defense against deforming influences or sudden shocking events. Neglect of the
baby or *small child* by his mother, overindulgence or exag-
gerated concern, incompetence, harshness or "bossiness," dis-
agreement between father and mother as to the upbringing
of the child, the projection onto the child of the parents'
complexes, lack of maturity, conflicts and marriage difficulties
on the part of the parents—all this and much more can become fixated in the child's mind in the form of lasting anxieties, inhibitions, defense reflexes, and so on. Healthy growth
is rendered impossible or misdirected, and some sectors of
the child's mind stagnate on infantile levels beyond which
they never develop.

Thus again, in the *growing child*, the balanced tension
between superego and instinctive impulses—an indispensable
condition for the gradual assumption of the superego within
that conscious welcoming of one's own spiritual finality which

we call conscience—can be upset by prolonged excesses or defects in education (parents or educators too authoritarian or too weak, unresolved Oedipus complex, etc.). Sudden *shocking events* which the tender psyche cannot yet take in and assimilate may have a traumatic effect, greatly hinder or wholly paralyze spiritual growth and even produce regressions and a reactivation of previous stages of development. All these influences explain why, time and time again, maturing behavior may be disturbed by *infantile* reactions (such as belong to previous stages of development). Thus the whole psychic substratum of conscience may grow out of kilter, becoming for the seemingly adult conscience a prison from which it finds no release or a slope on which it stands or advances with immense difficulty.

Such *neurotic complexes*—as they are usually called—act as unfailingly and efficiently on the free will as a brain injury or a narcotic. They totally escape the individual's consciousness, making their influence prevail out of the unconscious on what he supposes to be normal, freely performed actions. They cannot be laid bare through rational insight or eliminated by means of the usual educational methods. Their presence increases the influence of the other inhibiting factors —bodily disturbances have stronger repercussions on a disturbed psyche and are, in their turn, aggravated by the psychic trouble. The social influences too often find a welcome ally in unconscious anxieties, resentments or repressed feelings.

Frequently these complexes stay hidden under an apparent equilibrium. In fact they are not harmoniously integrated within the total personality, but consciousness has tried to assimilate them by finding all kinds of valid reasons for the actions they inspire, by what is usually called "rationalization."

When we speak of a "neurotic personality" we create the impression that we are treating of an exceptional case of illness. In reality, every process of education, even the most excellent, is so deficient, the vulnerability of the young mind so much threatened by the factual situation, that the harmoniously integrated personality is somewhat of an exception, may also look like a "limit." The average individual, even if not neurotic, lives continually under the influence of *neuroticizing factors*. He has to live with a host of unassimilated deformations, tyrannical automatisms, paralyzing anxieties, obsessive impulses or hungry frustrations, vague feelings of guilt, defense reactions or aggressive reflexes, acting out of the unconscious on the adult decisions time and time again with infantile taboo threats and taboo rebellions, thus pulling them down more or less to the instinctive level.

That in our times these neuroticizing factors exert a stronger and wider-ranging influence than in the past is generally admitted. It is *more difficult* for today's young people to develop an authentic *adult commitment to life*. Young people are getting an earlier start in adult life while, at the same time, their opportunity for assuming the risks of adult occupations is deferred. This considerably increases the danger of a blasé grown-up infantilism. This process is the result of a variety of factors, such as, to mention only a few: the growing disintegration of many families, the almost complete undermining of the father image in education and the rapid evolution of our civilization towards some kind of pedagogical matriarchate; the fact that public assistance and the accepted level of living conditions is adapted to the small family with one or two children and the gradual modeling of the whole educational process according to the "only child" standard; the precocious physical puberty with the prolonged time of confusion between bodily and spiritual maturity which ensues; the widening gap between an overindulgent education aimed at full security and the harsher claims of task and profes-

sion, between external cultural comfort and interior spiritual culture; the uncertainty of a time of "mutation" in which
society, lacking a universally accepted ideal type, is in quest
of its own future image of man; the voyeurism of a civilization
which supplies an abundance of information without corresponding possibilities for a critical sifting of its value; the
aiming of propaganda and advertising at the younger section
of the public—the future customers—with concentration on
their more expensive infantile needs—all these and many more
factors militate against a well-balanced and harmonious
growth into adulthood.

If we add up all these factors which hinder human freedom,
the outlook is at first glance very unpropitious so far as human
responsibility is concerned, and hence also the notion of sin.
Not only the psychically disturbed person, but also one who
considers himself normal and is so considered by others, is
not as free as he might *wish* to be; he does not always do
what he wants to do. He is not even as free as an onlooker
might think, seeing him in action; he does not always do what
the *others* think he is doing. He is not even as free as he
himself often believes. Expressions like "I knew what I was
doing" and "I did it on purpose" are not always reliable yard-
sticks for the real extent of freedom with which some actions
are performed; man does not always do what *he himself* thinks
he is doing.

Does it not follow that the notion of sin, and especially the
notion of mortal sin committed with "full advertence and full
consent," becomes very problematic? Must we not earnestly
ask the question: Are we really *free enough* to sin in the sense
which traditional moral teaching attaches to that word? From
the point of view of taboo morality, man is almost continually
"transgressing." Man's helplessness before the objective good
is a datum which must be taken into account in our moral

and religious life. Of this there is no doubt. But the question is: Are we morally and religiously responsible for that helplessness? Does not what we call sin always in fact issue from the immature in us, the socially unadapted—from the fact that we are unable to assimilate our past? Does it not derive from those sectors of the mind which are still stagnating on an instinctive level, which thus hinder the unfolding of our freedom? Would not every human being be good and behave well if the effects of all the mistakes made in his education were corrected, if he were delivered from all complexes, relieved of the crushing pressure of society? Might it not be true in this sense that man's free will always strives towards the good and that only his lack of freedom is responsible for what we call his sin? In that case we could no longer call the sinner guilty, but only sick or immature. And in that event, treating or judging him as guilty would imply that society, or the Church, in its turn, judged not on the basis of mature insight but according to infantile taboo criteria.

ELEMENTS OF A SOLUTION

A satisfactory answer to all these questions can be given only on the basis of a renewed and revised concept of the structure of human freedom.

FUNDAMENTAL OPTION AND OBJECT CHOICE

It is generally said of our freedom that it is a freedom of choice. That is correct, but the expression can be misunderstood. Not every choice involves the kind of freedom man has. Instinct likewise makes unpredictable choices continually, and even an electronic brain, responding to a small number of stimuli, can dictate to a robot reactions which are practically unpredictable and give to the observer without special competence in technology the impression that they are free. The choice in human activity becomes really a free choice only from the fact that it comes from a much deeper root than ordinary actions. That deeper source, too, is some kind of choice, not with respect to specific objects but with respect to the totality of existence, its meaning and its direction. In order to distinguish it from everyday object choices we prefer to speak of an *option*. The choice among the many objects offers an infinite number of possibilities; the fundamental option is made between a "yes" and a "no" in which man, as a spirit, unconditionally commits or refuses himself. That option always amounts to letting oneself go: either yielding to a "becoming," to a growing towards a more perfect self-realization, or falling back on an already acquired self-possession, rejecting the advance in self-realization and the new risks. In order to realize itself this basic option must enter into a dialog with a complete psycho-physical situation and development, assume all acquired determinisms within its free directedness and thus bestow on them, out of that freedom, a new shape for the future. The continual object-choice which this entails will be a free choice only to the—often very restricted—extent in which it shares the freedom of the basic option. To this same extent the individual actions also share the responsibility which the basic option involves. Only to the extent of this participation can they be called either good actions or sins on the moral or religious levels.

This is not the place for philosophical proofs in support of this doctrine.[4] Yet there are in concrete human experience moments when we become conscious, as it were experimentally, of the clash between the fundamental option and the psycho-physical elements. For more frequently than one might think, a person's conscience enters into conflict with impulses he feels unable to master; he cannot do what he sincerely and firmly wants to do. The quality of the "moral" suffering that follows on such a clash is, as it were, an existential experience of the freedom of option.

True, one can produce a neurosis also in an animal by unsettling its conditioned reflexes in such a way that instinct loses its bearings. But the animal succumbs without defense to its helplessness, and one can rescue it only by re-educating its conditioned reflexes from without. Man suffers so much from his helplessness precisely because in him it conflicts with another reality. That other reality, which alone can render the helplessness conscious as helplessness, can only be a creative freedom. In quite a number of insane people suffering lacks this moral character, since they are no longer aware of their helplessness and their distress. Psychotherapy, on the other hand, becomes possible only through a steady appeal to the implicitly present creative liberty. Whether consciously used or resulting spontaneously from the circumstances, it is ultimately only a technique which gives the option of freedom the possibility of growing creatively through, and emerging from, the network of determinisms.

In Freudian psychoanalysis this appeal to freedom remains largely implicit. It is somewhat more explicit in the Jungian process of individuation. In more recent schools, such as the existential analysis of Frankl, the therapeutical praxis of Binswanger, Matussek and von Gebsattel, and even more in the non-directive therapy of Carl Rogers, an effort is made to enter into dialog with the deepest creative freedom.

That these methods aim at a fundamental option, and not at a freedom which always chooses the good, is evident from the profound anxiety with which the possibility of a breakthrough is at first experienced. The cure of the depressed and inhibited person is marked by a succession of moments in which he is aware of a rending of the network of determinisms and glimpses the road to real freedom lying open before him. In these moments he sees himself, in bare and immediate consciousness, placed before the painful dilemma: either to cling to the miserable but familiar, hence relatively safe, shelter of the infantile situation, or to summon up the courage to leave that shelter and to run the risk of a new birth.

In such moments man experiences his freedom concretely: the moral character of such an option is not in doubt, either for the person himself or for those who witness his struggle.

FREEDOM AND GRACE

On the level of the religious decision, within the relation of intimacy with God's inviting love, the same kind of freedom is at work. It is remarkable how the Christ of the gospels, who "knew what was in man" (Jn. 2.25),* takes our freedom for granted, yet refers again and again, beyond the particular decisions, to the deeper fundamental option as the thing that ultimately counts. Nowhere perhaps is that fundamental option brought out more sharply than in his words: "For he who would save his life will lose it; but he who loses his life for my sake will save it" (Mk. 8.35). In the shocking image of "take up his cross and follow me" (Mk. 8.34) the unconditional character of the risk which is to be assumed, the fundamental nature of the choice which is to be made, is plunged into glaring light. Equally unconditional is the commitment which is demanded in the "seek ye first the kingdom of God and his justice"; what follows: "And all these things shall be

---

* The scriptural quotations in this book are from *The Holy Bible,* Confraternity Edition. Copyright 1962 The Confraternity of Christian Doctrine.

given to you besides" (Mt. 6.33) refers undoubtedly to the host of minor problems and particular decisions of everyday life. The parables of the treasure in the field, of the precious pearl for which one sells everything, make the same unconditional demand under their appealing imagery.

In the so frequently quoted parable of the talents, the servant who has opted for security and refused the decisive commitment is the only one who is condemned and punished. The case of the servant who, having staked everything, ultimately failed and lost everything, is not mentioned in the parable. It is as if, in the Kingdom of God, whoever has the courage to commit himself unconditionally is never defrauded and never loses, even if in his daily life he may meet with much bad luck and many defeats.

Finally, the conflict between the basic choice and temporary powerlessness is illustrated more sharply, in a short, rarely quoted parable of the Gospel of St. Matthew, where Jesus speaks against the scornful and merely exterior judgments of the Pharisees: " 'But what do you think? A man had two sons; and he came to the first and said, "Son, go and work today in my vineyard." But he answered and said, "I will not"; but afterwards he regretted it and went. And he came to the other and spoke in the same manner. And this one answered, "I go, sir"; but he did not go. Which of the two did the father's will?' They said, 'The first.' Jesus said to them, 'Amen I say to you, the publicans and harlots are entering the kingdom of God before you.' " (Mt. 21.28–31)

SIN UNTO DEATH, MORTAL AND VENIAL SIN

In this perspective it is perhaps possible to sift *particular actions* according to their moral significance and to discover the exact bearing of the classic distinction between *venial sin* and *mortal sin.*

Human action is situated historically. The fundamental option of liberty cannot be expressed adequately in one single action. Every action is at once an expression and a restriction of man's basic choice; free self-realization is broken up in the progression of a temporal development. It must find a path across a complete psycho-physical situation and history, and it must realize itself within human interrelatedness in a world which has already been constructed by the consciousness and the freedom of others. Only in the action which brings man's existence to its term and condenses it into a meaningful destiny, in the act of dying—an action performed on the boundary between time and eternity, standing within time but opting with man's whole existence for an eternity—only in that action can our freedom utter itself completely in an all-embracing fundamental option.

The fact that our particular actions are situated historically explains why they are never wholly free, why they never express our full freedom, but only *share* that freedom to a greater or lesser extent. Some of these actions will be mainly *reflexes,* instinctive reactions, routine activities drilled in by education. Yet even these actions never wholly escape the influence of freedom, because the habitual paths, although laid out by education and circumstances before any use of freedom, are later in life freely embraced or rejected, and thus assumed to some extent within free self-realization.

Other actions constitute *peak moments,* decisive instants— *"kairos,"* the hour of man's life, as Scripture calls it—crossroads where freedom chooses a direction and determines its attitude for a whole stage, perhaps even for the whole remainder, of life. Sometimes the external action symbolizes, through its solemnity, the decisive character of the choice performed: conversion, marriage, ordination, vows, etc. But it is possible also that the external solemnity of such moments does not coincide with the internal decision, and that the latter occurs at a quite different moment, on the occasion of an unimportant or apparently routine event. In how many marriages, for example, does the consent given, however sincerely and validly, at the altar, confront the partners only much later, in a moment of total sincerity when they painfully face each other, with the choice: whether to seal it into an unconditional commitment, or to allow it to degenerate into some kind of business compromise, or to make it henceforward into a perpetual lie.

Between the two extremes there is a whole range of possibilities in which freedom has a *gradually increasing share*. Within this range the moralists have tried to define certain zones. They have defined them, mainly in a negative way—for the evil choices made in them—by the terms *venial sin* and *mortal sin*. It is remarkable that there are no generally accepted terms for the corresponding good choices. When an action is such that a negative basic choice clearly manifests itself in it, we speak of mortal sin. If it is so superficial or so unfree that the basic option cannot really take shape in it, we speak of venial or excusable sin.

It is difficult to draw the boundary line between the two sorts of sins, because so many different elements are involved in them.

The action itself, in its materiality, may be so unimportant or peripheral that it is hard to see how a basic choice could express itself in it. Or it may be so momentous that we cannot imagine such an action not embodying the fundamental orientation of a human life. Moreover, the moment in the process of growth or maturation in which the action occurs, the symbolic value it can have in psychic terms, the way it affects man's relation to his fellow men—all this is of great importance if we wish to discover its real meaning.

As the moralists, for pedagogical reasons, have mainly felt a strong need for handy, clear and objective criteria, they have often insisted too onesidedly upon the materiality of the action and have made up their classification of sins almost exclusively on that basis. As a result, the notions of mortal sin and of venial sin have been so objectified in the consciousness of the average Christian, that it has become a matter of course to consider certain "things" as mortal sins. Is "this" or "that" a mortal sin or only a venial sin? This sort of question is frequently asked. In reaction against this trend some people are inclined to overemphasize the influence of the situation factors and demand for mortal sin such a total commitment that almost no human action fulfills these conditions. Possibly Fr. Schoonenberg[5] has discovered the right middle position through the distinction he makes between "mortal sin" and "sin unto death." The biblical expression "sin unto death" (1 Jn. 5.16ff.)—which he rightly equates with the Johannine "anomia" (injustice or wickedness, 1 Jn. 3.4) and the "sin against the Holy Spirit" of the gospel (Mk. 3.28ff. and par.)— is interpreted by him as *final impenitence,* the final choice which occurs in the act of dying. It is the last, the final sin. One who commits it is dead before God; he died, morally speaking, in sin, even if biologically he may survive for a while. By definition, however, this total commitment cannot be discovered in the course of this life, and if one puts as a condition for a mortal sin committed during life that absolute, conscious and total rejection of God, it is quite evident that man is unable to commit a real mortal sin. However, in the sense in which Schoonenberg understands *mortal sin*—as a rejection of God within a still provisional but important choice, deriving from a central option—it does occur, not as frequently as a rigid moral catalog would make us accept, but still as something which remains within the normal possibilities of a free human choice.

Even for the *child* the possibility of a "mortal sin" in that sense is not totally excluded. Even in the life of a child flashes of intense consciousness may occur, instants in which a seemingly childlike gesture is experienced as a transparent symbol for a decisive life orientation. It is true that such prefigurative moments of adulthood will only rarely coincide with those actions which a rigid moral codification brands as mortal sins even for children. Much more than on the sexual level, for instance, the possibility of committing a mortal sin will occur for the child within affective alternatives: love or hatred, self-donation or self-assertion, acceptance or refusal.

Until the quite recent past the case of the person *damned for one mortal sin* was a favorite theme for retreat masters. Transposed into the foregoing terminology, the question is: Is it possible that in the first single action through which a person turns away from God in a fundamental way, thus committing a "mortal sin," his basic option might be so radically and so totally expressed that this choice would decide the whole direction of his existence, becoming for him concretely a "sin unto death" within which his free will would forever assume its position? The possibility of such an action could be discussed indefinitely. In practice, however, the probability is so slight that one need hardly take it into account. The treatment of this theme in the pulpit is a good example of the deformation of the truths of the faith which takes place when discussion is allowed to degenerate into a mere game of concepts without any contact with reality. With the best of intentions hell, instead of being presented as the freely accepted, everlasting situation of the refusal of God, is mythologized into some kind of surprise roundup by the divine police of delinquents caught in the act—in their first robbery, for instance. Mortal sin is often materially conceived simply as doing something which is forbidden, with no account taken of circumstances or lack of experience which might make a really free choice impossible; instead of a moment within a development, it then becomes an autonomous event which automatically brings about its sanction, and which can only be undone by the almost equally isolated action (the countermove) of a confession. Such a shallow conception overlooks a few basic points: that a first wrong choice is generally neutralized, long before confession, by a new breakthrough of the basic option towards the good; that in the dialectics of the basic choice the attraction of the good is unusually strong and almost ineradicable; that the fear produced in the listener lest he should have decided with his deepest will against his deepest will is utterly senseless.

Mortal sin and venial sin occur on what we have called the moral level. Insofar as the moral task of self-realization is assumed within the *religious relationship*, both concepts and their distinction continue to apply. But we can no longer keep them as norms once we face the specific demands of the life of grace.

The fundamental refusal of that life, real *infidelity*, is a sin which has almost nothing in common with mortal sins on the moral level. For here the rejection no longer occurs after the manner characterizing the approach to a created reality. Now it is a question of breaking off all intercourse with God himself, as he addresses man without intermediary. Despite the mysterious nature of the act of faith, this rejection is essentially of the same order as the rejection of the beatific vision, of which faith, though in obscurity, is a real anticipation. That is why infidelity is a much closer approximation to the

"sin unto death" than to "mortal sin," although the fact that
the knowledge of faith is only "a confused reflection in a
mirror" explains why even infidelity cannot simply be equated
with the final impenitence of a God-rejecting death.

On the other hand, the life of grace offers possibilities
which rise so far above moral self-realization that they can
hardly be measured with the yardstick of moral obligation.
Ordering one's life in accordance with the evangelical coun-
sels, a vocation to the priesthood or to the religious life—all
this belongs to a sphere of intimacy and of deepest meeting
in love where we step out of context as soon as we use words
like "obligation," "must," and "sin"; where, on the contrary,
we can only speak of *invitation*, of proffered opportunity and
gentle prodding. Is it very meaningful to call the refusal of
such a vocation a sin, even a mortal sin? Is this not an application of the gross standards of moral concepts to a much
subtler reality? And would it not be more exact to say that in
love an invitation may be more binding than an order, and
coolness more wounding than betrayal? Man may not decide
arbitrarily whether to accept or reject a clearly recognized
divine vocation; he is bound, however, not merely by a moral
obligation, but because he has been elected in love. To speak
of "sin" in this context must be to use the word in a wholly
new meaning, with which the distinction between mortal and
venial sin is no longer commensurable.

THE TIME FACTOR

An important corollary of the fact that the development of
human freedom takes place in the context of history is that
the *time* factor is *essential* in this realization. Moral growth
does not occur at the pace of technical developments, in which
an effort is made to reduce the time element as far as possible

or even eliminate it altogether, but according to the rhythm of organic growth, slowly and gradually. Very often an important decision cannot be taken on the spot, it must come to a slow ripening out of the situation. And when the decision has ripened much time will often be needed to integrate the psychic resistances, the bonds of custom, the pressure of the environment and of the circumstances in such a way that the resolution can take historical shape in mature and harmonious activity. Modern man, under the spell of the demon of speed and push-button technique, finds it very hard to adapt himself to that slow rhythm. The outboard motor appeals to him more than the sailboat, in which he must continually watch and respond to his sail, the wind and the water. Even in the matter of his own growth his impatience makes him all too often rebel against the temporary powerlessness of his will.

This slow or gradual growth is even more characteristic of the *religious level,* on which the vocation to grace must make its way in a life that is weakened and dislocated through its heredity and by concupiscence. No wonder, then, if Christ himself has emphasized that law of gradualness in his teaching.

The parables of the leaven, the mustard seed and so many others point in the same direction. Christ's attitude towards the obtuseness and the initial lack of understanding on the part of his apostles, his utterances about his own "hour" for which he must wait, can be wholly understood only through an awareness of the proper rhythm of human life and of grace.

CAN WE JUDGE?

If all we have said about the relation between external action and internal free decision is true, it follows that although the external action has some connection with the inner decision which is its origin, it is very difficult to interpret that relation correctly. It is often asserted that the outer action is the *sign* of the inner decision. But the word sign might be somewhat too precise; a sign has a clear, univocal relation to a signified reality. The outer human action, on the other hand, is so polyvalent as a sign that it might be better to call it the *symptom* of the inner decision.[6] To yield its real meaning a symptom must always be seen within a totality of converging indications. Let us take an everyday example. The fact that people do not attend Sunday Mass may be the sign of a loss of faith. But it may derive from countless other causes which have often nothing in common with real loss of faith. It may even indicate a transition to a more profound faith. Thus again, masturbation may be the sign of an emerging sensuality not yet integrated within the total personality. But it may also be the manifestation of existential anxiety, or affective frustration, or helpless rebellion, or masochism. It is not an illness but a symptom, as polyvalent as fever in a sick body.

The real meaning of the symptom the sinful action is can be discovered only when we can go down to the root of the decision and, as it were, *coincide with the basic option* which embodies itself in that action, so that from that perspective we can measure the resistances and determinisms this option has met on its road to realization. Only then could we exactly gauge the degree of responsibility and of guilt. Therefore, as far as others are concerned, we can get to know hardly anything about the deeper ground of their actions. We are reduced to assuming, surmising and guessing, and we shall consistently err if we consider only the outer facts. This is strikingly demonstrated by the continual differences of opinion between judges and psychiatrists in criminal cases. Their often diametrically opposed judgments concerning the degree of accountability of the accused person arise not only from wholly different interpretations of the external phenomena but also from fundamentally different views with regard to the very notion of accountability. And here only juridical responsibility is involved; the judgment does not touch the problem of moral guilt.

Equally striking evidence is to be found in the fact that the method of questionnaires and statistical opinion polling is almost wholly unsuccessful in penetrating into the sphere of man's intimacy to unravel the deeper motives of his attitudes.

Modern man has become much more prudent, too, when it comes to asserting that he *knows himself*. For he is aware that he always looks at himself through the prism of the whole present situation, and he realizes how subtle the role of self-deception is. A spectroscope, which would analyze in him the innermost play of light and shadow, should aim more at an *"examen d'inconscience"* than at the usual examination of conscience. And even then the judgment about oneself and the free decision which that judgment encounters would be seen to lie at such a depth that one might perhaps experience the freedom existentially but could not objectivate it as a concrete and measurable quantity. Awareness of the large measure of determinism in his free activity and of the great influence of his subjectivity on the *imago* he holds of himself and of others forbids modern man to remain on the surface of his "ego"; he must coincide with his deeper "self" in a movement of recollection. He must leave the sphere of matter-of-fact—which he prefers on account of its so-called objectivity —and plunge into the much more central sphere of the "heart," whence the authentic decisions emerge and where real freedom gropes for its direction. Thus, paradoxically, the realization of one's own lack of freedom may point the way not only towards a deeper self-knowledge, but also towards a more authentic unfolding of that freedom and a gradual increase of the freedom of mankind. This leads us to vistas of the future such as Teilhard de Chardin has so persuasively sketched.

APPLICATIONS TO THE PASTORAL DOMAIN

The modified conception of the freedom of man's sinful actions must involve thorough changes of perspective in the pastoral approach to sinful man. A first series of questions concerns the integration of these new insights within the dogmatic and pastoral theology of the sacrament of penance. A second series concerns the situation of sinful man within the life of the Church.

SIN AND CONFESSION

The question arises spontaneously: If it is true that man can know his own sinfulness only in a very imperfect way, what can be the meaning of the penitent's detailed confession, as required by the Church, of the species, number and aggravating circumstances of his sins? How can the priest, on the other hand, judge the penitent's dispositions, in order to give or refuse him absolution? What advice can he give him, and what may he demand in the matter of specific occasions of sin?

A first global answer to that question might be: The new realization of man's psychic complexity may force both priest and penitent to see and experience confession more integrally again in its *sacramentality*.[7]

The Council of Trent has proposed as a point of faith that the absolution in confession is an *"actus judicialis"* (the sentence of a judge). From the context and the comments of the Fathers it is clear that this meant two things. First, that the absolution does not consist in a mere praying together of confessor and penitent for God's forgiveness, or in a mere acknowledgement and declaration that God forgives the penitent's sin if the sinner really believes in that forgiveness. Absolution is an efficacious sign which really causes that forgiveness. Secondly, that the meeting which occurs in confession is entered into by a Christian, a member of Christ's Church; hence that it can take place solely within the ambit and through the intermediary of the Church, the only and indispensable link and meeting place between the Christian and Christ. This assumes that the sinner confesses and submits not only his sinfulness but also his sins to the Church, and that in absolving the priest exercises a judicial power over sin, as given by Christ to his Church—i.e., that he acts as a real and efficient mediator between the sinful Christian and Christ who has risen and triumphed over sin.

Like many other points of faith, the idea of the *actus judicialis* has been *oversystematized* by a too conceptualistic theology, out of its context, and without any reference to the analogy of faith. The whole content of the secular concept of judicial power is applied to confession: the detailed brief of the facts, the careful questioning of the defendant, the inquiry into his accountability and inner dispositions, the placing of safeguards for his future behavior—all these elements of the secular court system are applied—often literally applied—to confession, as if it were a juridical verdict or a ruling in response to a petition for clemency. And the ordinary catechetical teaching saw to it that this bureaucratic theology should grow even more rigid in ready-made tables of mortal and venial sin, in confession guides for all circumstances and all states of life and in a casuistry laboriously worked out into the minutest details.

In all this something was in danger of being lost, something too often was forgotten: the most essential element of the sacramental action, the fact that it is a *sign*. The accent was put so emphatically on the material exactness of the submitted account of sins that one overlooked how the meeting of confession and absolution is only a sign of a much profounder meeting between the sinner and the loving judgment of God, as embodied unto eternal mercy in Christ, and how the mediation of the Church receives from that loving judgment its only meaning, hence also its limitations. The present Council feels this so strongly that it stipulates in its Constitution on the Liturgy: "The rite and the texts of confession must be revised in such a way that they express more clearly the proper nature and the effect of that sacrament" (n. 72).

1. The Confession of Sins

Among the deep-seated causes of the present crisis in the sacrament of penance, the confession of sins as it is practiced today is a very specific difficulty. If so many people reject sacramental confession and long to cast off their sinfulness in a direct meeting with God, the reason is not so much that they no longer feel the need for a visible sign. Confessing one's guilt is an archetypal experience, one so deeply anchored in the very structure of the human psyche that the need for it will never disappear. But modern man no longer sees in the confession of sins as practiced in the sacrament of penance a real "signifying" of his guilt. And that authenticity has vanished because the materiality of the sign has been so much stressed, endowed with such autonomy, that it absorbs the whole attention, leaving no scope for the "signification."

Awareness of the psychic complexity of the sinful action may force us to experience the confession of sins more authentically as the sign that it is. The priest in the confessional is no public attorney looking for an exact reconstruction of the crime, nor is he a psychiatrist who must decide how accountable the defendant is or a psychotherapist who must rid the penitent of his complexes and his unconscious inhibitions. He is one who, in God's name, utters God's releasing word over the sin. What he must know and what the penitent must tell him is not an adequate description of the sinner's situation, a perfectly true insight into the extent of his sinfulness. What the penitent tells him is only a sign of what he tells God. The *confession of sins* is a sincere *signifying*, to the extent of his insight and according to certain rules prescribed by the Church, of his being a sinner before God. Hence he confesses more (or often, unknowingly, much less) than what he expresses in words. The sins he confesses are only a sign and a very imperfect expression of what God forgives him. And the *priest's judgment*, his human meeting with this sinfulness, is only a *sign*—often a very imperfect and shadowy sign—of the merciful salvific judgment of God, which is not tied to the limitations and mistakes of our human judgment. Both penitent and priest may be wrong in their judgment about the confessed sins; in fact they often are—much more often than our textbooks of moral theology suppose. If both are in good faith, this mistake does not matter at all, for God forgives not what has been confessed, but what has been signified by the confession.

However various the forms in which the sacrament of penance has taken shape within the Church over the centuries, they all have one point in common: they always comprise a "signifying" confession by the sinning member of the Church, not only of his sinfulness in general, but of the sins he personally has committed. Hence the Council of Trent declares that by divine disposition this "signifying" belongs to the essence of the sacrament (although the expression *jure divino* had not yet acquired the meaning we assign to it today and was often used for ecclesiastical and even for civil laws).

The very detailed norms for that signifying were first laid down by the Council of Trent and have since been impressed upon the faithful: all mortal sins must be confessed with species and number and also with any circumstances which might modify the nature of the sin. Yet, despite every tendency towards rigidity, even textbook teaching retained enough feeling for the "signifying" function of confession to acknowledge the right of confessor and penitent to deviate from the material completeness of the confession *if that completeness would impair the signifying function* instead of promoting it. Thus, in the case of the scrupulous penitent, whose anxiety about completeness threatens to smother the religious meaning of the confession of sins. Also for sick or dying persons, whose state of exhaustion makes it desirable that the whole attention and all available spiritual energy should be devoted to a contrite resignation rather than a painstaking effort of memory. Or, again, for the penitent whose relationship to the confessor (member of his family, close collaborator, superior) is such that the human resonances of the confession of some sins would clash too disturbingly with the religious meaning of the act. Should the penitent himself stand in a sinful relation to the confessor, the Church even forbids confession under the most severe penalties, because in such a case the sign cannot possibly reach the required integrity of signification.

Might not a return to a more authentic experiencing of the sign-value of the confession of sins mean for countless people not only a release but also a growth towards religious authenticity? Might they not recover with greater integrity the meaning of confession as a salvific meeting with Christ within the Church, if their examination of conscience were centered in Christ's welcoming love rather than in themselves? The objection to the examination of conscience expressed by a profoundly religious man—"They think they will forget themselves by dint of looking at themselves"—can be met and answered only through such a reorientation of the sacrament towards God.

On the priest's side, too, might not many a confession be better if the *questioning* were inspired not so much by an anxious solicitude for a materially complete enumeration of sins as by the need to allow the penitent to express as authentically as he can his personal awareness of sin? The questioning might then become more discreet, with a more sensitive respect for the person; it might become the exception rather than the rule, and it would not, as often happens now, destroy rather than promote the authentic sign value of the confession of sins.

Might this not also supply an encouraging solution for the countless *"Easter only"* confessions of people who are so underdeveloped religiously that what may perhaps be a vivid awareness of sin can hardly pierce the crust of psychic inhibitions, human respect and secretiveness, and whose confession can be as awkward, yet as eloquent, a sign as the clumsy gestures of their friendship or the stammering words of their declarations of love? It might equally be a welcome solution for the confession practice among *non-Westerners;* for some highly cultivated Asiatic peoples, for instance, whose whole way of thinking and whose feeling for symbolism is offended by confession in the Western manner.

It is especially in the *devotional confession* that the problem of the acknowledgment of sins would be considerably aided by a stronger emphasis on the religious sign-value. Where there are no mortal sins to be confessed, there can be no material norm for the confessing of sins. It is guided exclusively by the desire to express, as integrally as possible, the need of meeting the risen Christ with one's burden of sin. The recurrent complaint, "I don't know what to say," or "It's always the same," does not necessarily point to shallowness or lack of self-knowledge; it may equally well be the expression of religious sincerity and a deeper realization of human complexity. The more we experience our sinfulness, the more we also notice the inextricable blending in us of the wheat and the cockle which are to grow together until the final harvest; the more difficult, too, it becomes to express in facts and figures all that is unutterable and unfathomable in ourselves: our inner disorder; the labyrinthine ways of evil in our soul; the tacit compromises with our own cowardice or the conniving acquiescence in that which leads into sin; our refusal to commit ourselves and our pretexts for sloth; our running away from God into dissipation and our attempts to ransom ourselves with devotional practices; the way we ration our generosity and our love of neighbor. The difficulty lies deeper than we generally admit.

The solution for this difficulty should amount to more than technical devices. We are often advised to "personalize" our confessions. This expression is ambiguous. It is often interpreted as a psychological scrutiny, a more exact analysis of our actions. That easily leads to a "psychologizing" of confession, which, to my mind, may have very harmful consequences. When we read some—especially Dutch—books and what they present as a model confession we sometimes wonder whether we have to do with a confession or with a psychological pep talk, and we ask ourselves what function, if any, the final absolution might have in all this.[8] The whole attention is directed towards the subject himself, and if, after a while, the

results of confession are no longer psychologically noticeable—
this is almost unavoidable in the event of a deeper religious
development—the devotional confession will readily be dis-
continued as devoid of value.

The *personalizing* of the confession of sins should be attempted not so much along the lines of a psychological clarification of what must be said as in a renewed stress on a more
authentic and profound realization of the sign-value of what
is said and on the quality of the *awareness of sinfulness* which
expresses itself in that confession. When someone in his examination of conscience, without any effort to fathom his actions
in their deeper psychological motivation, succeeds in living
his past in religious recollection, out of the deepest root of
his being-for-God, there is a good hope that the connaturality
of his faith and love with the divine exigency proposed to his
life will begin to function as a power of discrimination which
will existentially, not psychologically, sift the authentic from
the unauthentic elements of his spiritual life.

That line of demarcation will be more difficult to verbalize
than a psychological analysis. There are great individual differences in this respect: some people are more eloquent than
others; some are extroverts, others introverts; there are many
other factors at work. Hence, in the concrete confession of
sins, this inner realization will be expressed quite differently
by different penitents—by some in vivid terms, by others in
plain, or even in stereotyped, hardly ever changing formulas.
Possibly, as the inner life grows stronger, the same phenomenon may occur for the confession of sins as happens in
prayer: it becomes increasingly poor in ideas and in words,
it condenses its fullness in a seemingly commonplace expression which nevertheless is for the person in question filled
with the plenitude of his experience of life and of God. An

attentive listener will be able to detect, within the poverty of such a confession, the unmistakable note of *religious authenticity*.

When this innermost need of God's saving and purifying presence, the meeting with Christ who has risen and triumphed over sin, is always experienced in living authenticity, less importance will be attached to the psychologically visible results of frequent confession. The routine of an ever returning, almost changeless symbolism will then express and nourish the growing vital intimacy with God, just as the monotonous routine of common life and of loving communion between husband and wife serves as the growing and living symbol of all the seasons of married love. Quite often—more often than psychologists tend to believe—this regularly repeated coinciding with his true self and with the core of his relation with Christ will lead a man even psychologically into decisive moments of breakthrough and prepare the way for a gradual integration even of his psychic immaturities.

2. The Address of the Priest

The same difficulty the penitent has in the confession of sins attends the *address* of the confessor. This address, too, is an intra-sacramental event, and not, in the first instance, an occasion for moral or psychological counseling. What absolution will accomplish in the sinner is anticipated liturgically in the priest's address. It is therefore a sign of the concrete appeal of a merciful God, creating a new life, but also inviting, urging, demanding; of a God who is to meet, in Christ and in the Church, this concrete sinner in his concrete sinfulness.

The priest may use this religiously very intimate moment to give practical advice, to propose certain things, to help develop insight into the problem created by the situation. The function of spiritual direction and moral counseling may be exercised on the occasion of confession.

Yet this function has nothing to do with confession as such, even though historically it has often been associated with it. Furthermore, the priest will not, in most instances, have gathered enough information from the penitent to give safe psychological guidance without endangering the religious character of confession through a long conversation mainly profane in content. A directive given with the best intention, but based on inadequate information, may have exactly the opposite effect, and the penitent, who mistakenly includes it in the sacred content of the sacrament, will often be afraid of disobeying it, lest he should refuse to do what the sacrament itself demands. Thus innumerable conflicts of conscience originate in the platitudes uttered too hastily for complex situations by a well-meaning confessor. Aversion to a conversation forced on him in confession, anxiety about a too human curiosity trying to pry into his intimate affairs, put a damper on many a Christian's enthusiasm for the sacrament of penance and make him unwilling to use it.

Modern man wants to receive this sacrament again in its religious integrity, and we must satisfy his need. This makes it desirable that *confession* and eventual *spiritual direction* should be carefully kept *apart* wherever possible, and that psychological counseling should take place outside the confessional.

From this point of view the restoration of a *collective liturgical celebration of confession* which, while maintaining the present practice of confession, links it once more with the valuable elements of ancient tradition is to be welcomed as a step forward.[9] Here the danger of psychologizing is reduced to a minimum. The biblical context and the atmosphere of prayer deflect the examination of conscience from excessive attention to self and lead it into a God-centered perspective. The ecclesial dimension of sin and forgiveness is emphasized in a strong and releasing manner. And the priest's address becomes the message of God's merciful Word, in the presence of which man cannot help taking up his position on the religious level. The results of this renovation point to an often amazed rediscovery by the faithful of the ecclesial and sacramental meaning of confession, which appears to have been pushed into the background in their former practice of the sacrament.

3. The "Firm Purpose of Amendment"

Can the same principle of sacramentality that frees confessor and penitent alike from an atmosphere of psychologizing self-analysis be applied to one more function of the absolving priest, that of ascertaining the dispositions of the penitent, especially the authenticity of his contrition and his so-called "firm purpose of amendment"? At first glance it looks very much as if in this area the personal psychological intuition of the priest should prevail. Yet, here too, only a purely religious attitude can safeguard the reverence due to the penitent's intimate life and to the hidden nature of the action of God's grace.

As the Church's representative, the priest who celebrates the sacrament of penance is obliged, as in the case of every other sacrament, to see to it that it is conferred in a valid and worthy manner. When he is faced with manifest bad faith or a mocking of the sacrament, he is confronted by the penitent himself with the impossibility of accomplishing his mediating task, and the refusal of absolution will only note this impossibility and prevent a useless profanation. In all other cases he will have to consider the very fact that someone comes to the sacrament as a very serious presumption of sincere contrition and of a decision to break with sin. A mere psychologically justified suspicion that contrition is not sufficient or the will not resolute enough has so much chance of being wrong that it would be unwarranted to let the granting of absolution depend on such an uncertain insight. The expressions and *formulas* which the penitent uses are mostly borrowed from what he has heard in catechism lessons and sermons about perfect and imperfect contrition, about the motivation for contrition, and about the conditions of an authentic purpose of amendment. Yet these formulas often hide a personal *experience* of a quite different nature from what they mean in scholastic terminology. "I can't really be sorry for it" may mean, for instance, that he cannot overlook the beautiful human aspects of a sinful adventure, while previous education has taught him so consistently to identify what is humanly repellent and shocking with what is sinful that he is unable to distinguish the sinful from the beautiful aspects of the adventure with any degree of clarity. "As soon as I get the chance, I'll do it again" may be a clumsy way of expressing the combination of sincere will with a feeling of at least temporary powerlessness for good. In both cases an anxiety is expressed which can only derive from a sincere will for good, and is a guarantee both of the contrition and of the firm resolve. I still remember the conclusion of a long conversation I had:—"I should like to confess all the things I have told you, but I'm afraid that I have no real contrition. Actually I don't feel at all sorry for it. I want to go to confession only out of a great anxiety." "Anxiety about what?" "About hell, of course." "And what, in the prospect of hell, are you so much afraid of? Pain or something?"—"Not at all, that leaves me cold. But never again to know oneself loved by God. . . . I can't bear the thought!" "Wouldn't what you have told me be an act of perfect contrition?"

The priest will often face the task of kindling and deepening a *contrition* which is still wavering and *immature*. If he tries to effect this through the psychological shock of a sharp rebuke or by insisting on the gravity and ugliness of the sin committed he will, as a rule, only evoke self-defense or hurt the penitent uselessly. Real contrition derives from love, not from horror of the evil in us. Making the penitent aware of God's love, inviting and waiting for him, tapping the *religious sources* of contrition, will offer much greater hope of a real inner change. What good can be expected from using the word "crime" or even "murder" for an abortion? Will not the awareness that God loved that burgeoning life, that one's own anxiety or egoism has been put above God's love, and that God's forgiveness means precisely an invitation to a greater and more selfless love for others in the future, penetrate more deeply to the "heart" and give hope of bringing about a more real conversion than words which render the anxiously hidden but deeply burning sense of guilt even more oppressive? Would not an engaged couple who have gone astray find more strength if they were made to realize that they have loved each other not too much but, in reality, too little—not with the fullness of love which God's love asked from them—more than if they are rebuked for their sensuality or threatened with a loss of future married happiness?

As for the firm purpose of amendment in the case of regular and almost changeless *relapsing* into the same sins, it presents penitent and confessor with a twofold question: whether the deeper groping underlying that series of sins is striving towards God or away from him, and whether the steady return of the same sins may not indicate that the root of the evil lies elsewhere than in the sins themselves, so that only an effort made on that deeper level might bring about a steady improvement.

The first question brings us back to what has been said of the basic option, and especially of the indispensable role of time in the breakthrough of that option across all that man is and has become psycho-physically. Between abstract *knowledge* of one's situation or of the solution to a problem and an *insight* which has become existentially real there is a gap which cannot be bridged by reasoning and arguments, but only by a hidden organic process of maturation, in patience and over a length of time. The process is rather like that of a hidden spring seeking an outlet through all the resistances of the soil, until suddenly it spurts freely, as spontaneously as if it had just come into existence on the spot: so the path of a *decision,* taken in all sincerity but still not well enough rooted in life, strives towards the *moment of a breakthrough,* when man can commit himself entirely in the resolution he has made. The same series of sinful acts, remaining apparently unchanged may, in two different persons, or even in the same person at different moments of his existence, have a totally different *value as a symptom.* It is true that the priest may use his psychological power of insight to find out whether, under the sinful symptoms, he can make out the first faint indications of an impending deliverance. He may sometimes, or even frequently, see the same unchanging sin turn from negative to positive through a gradual reorientation of the deeper directedness.

But equally often he is in danger of being wrong and of taking for ill-will what is only a temporary helplessness on the part of the penitent—or perhaps even his own impatience for a solution. The penitent who tells his confessor: "I'm giving up, I'm not going to fight anymore, I can no longer believe that God is helping me" does not expect the confessor to attack his ill-will, he is expecting some answer from God's mercy to what may sound like rebellion but is in fact an urgent and generally hopeful prayer for help. Experience shows only too clearly how often a religiously unauthentic answer from the priest, and even more a stern rebuke or the threat of refusing absolution, has had fateful consequences for the religious life of a penitent.

Once more, the only solution which respects the sacramentality of the confession can be found in a purely religious testing, by the *penitent himself*, of his good will as manifested in words against his inner essential directedness towards God. His firm resolve is not a merely autonomous psychological decision but an answer to God's merciful forgiveness, a readiness to allow the risen Christ, the conqueror of sin, to cure him of his sinful attachment. If the priest wants to promote this readiness, his dialog with the penitent may not be the meeting of his personal insight with the penitent's actual self-knowledge, but his attitude must be as integrally as possible a *referring to Christ's invitation,* which overcomes all sin. Then the penitent's answer can also come from his deepest readiness, which will act as a power of discrimination revealing either the sincerity of the psychological decision or the self-deception in it. The priest's psychological power of insight can be useful, because it may help him address the penitent in a religious language attuned to his dispositions. But it should not induce him to allow that address itself to turn into psychological counseling.

This gives us an answer to our second question also. If the root of the evil is deeper than the confessed sins, the power of discrimination deriving from the inner directedness towards God, precisely because it surges out of the innermost layers of the personality, will offer more hope, as it breaks through to the surface, of meeting and illuminating the hidden resistances than would a premature and unavoidably superficial probing for psychological drives and unconscious motivations.

4. The Sacramental Penance

This perspective likewise puts the *sacramental penance* in a truer light. Penance aims at reparation. It is true that, once forgiven, the sins need no longer be atoned for. But their consequences in the psyche and in the environment: the person himself with his weakened will, his greater attachment to evil; the sedimentation of the past in habits, reflexes and memories; the wrath and the pain of those who have been injured—all this demands, even after forgiveness, an effort at reparation and renovation. Classical theology calls this the *"reatus poenae,"* remaining in the sinner after confession. The sacramental penance is *not the fulfillment, but the sign* of this attempt at reparation. And the fact that it is not chosen by the penitent but imposed by the confessor is an expression of the fact that it is not an autonomous will of redress but an answer to the love of the risen Christ, the conqueror of sin, calling man to a new life. Hence in the penance too it is not the material act which is most important, but its value as a symbol of Christ's desire for renovation and of the sinner's willingness to meet that desire. The "proportion" of the penance with the sins committed, which is demanded by textbook theology, cannot be a real, but is only a symbolic proportion. A materially exiguous penance may, in some cases, have a more intense value as a symbol than a more extensive expiation. There is furthermore no objection to some intervention on the part of the penitent in determining the penance. A dialog may help in finding the best-adapted sign, or the penitent himself may be entrusted with the task of determining the sign which will appeal to him most. All this supposes, of course, that this looking for the sign occurs in the religious perspective which is so purely situated by the prayer recited by the absolving priest: "May the passion of Our Lord Jesus

Christ, the merits of the Blessed Virgin Mary and of all the saints, and also whatever good you do and evil you endure bring about the remission of your sins, an increase of grace, and the reward of everlasting life."

5. The "Proximate Occasion"

A delicate point in the formation of a firm purpose of amendment is the resolution to avoid the *proximate occasions* of sin. That notion of a "proximate occasion," too, has become so rigid during the last century that it has turned into a computation of probabilities and become synonymous with "serious risk." Ratings of movies, appraisals of books and of plays, are classic examples, and everybody knows how absolutely these only very approximate norms have been applied and are still being applied. Whereas the proximate occasion is in fact nothing but a *concrete situation* in which the occurrence of sin may be foreseen with moral certitude, always assuming that objective and subjective factors shall be taken into account—and not only objectivated subjective factors such as ability, habit, and so on, but the whole concrete situation of the person in question—in practice only the *objective probability* was considered. Thus, for instance, a married man entangled in an extra-marital affair was supposed to stand in a "free"—that is, avoidable—proximate occasion of sin, and he had to break with it unconditionally and at once. This is indeed the only solution in the majority of cases. But is the following case totally imaginary? Two people have sinned together, both desire to get out of this situation, but they realize that they can reach a real liberty and gradually grow back toward a new discovery of their own married love only if they succeed in fully willing, freely welcoming, consciously wresting from each other their definitive separation. They intend this sincerely, but they also know that during the encounters, in which they will have to accept in the spirit their mutual sacrifice and learn to grant each other their respective freedom, the immaturity of their decision will more than once manifest itself in weaknesses, maybe in a serious relapse. Yet they know equally well that a simple rupture would mean, for both of them, to run away from a struggle they would have to undergo again in other, more unfavorable circumstances, or one they would never be able to fight through to the finish, to the great detriment of their married life and of their own personal fulfillment. Are these people exposing themselves to a "proximate occasion" of sin, and should the possibility of finding an authentic solution to their situation be denied them on account of the danger involved? Once more, such cases are rather exceptional. But they do occur, and are possibly more frequent than a hasty, superficial judgment would suppose. The victory over sin which may be achieved in this way appears to be more lasting; a married happiness, previously battered, reconquered now after a hard struggle, manifests, by its depth and authenticity, the maturity of the decision which has finally been reached. Knowing, as we do, how complex a reality the human will is, and how much bound to time, we might, not modify, but bring back to its *original authenticity*, the very idea of the proximate occasion.

Would the priest, in this instance too, not safeguard confession more integrally as an encounter and as sign if, instead of deciding with his own fallible insight what is a proximate occasion for the penitent, he helped the penitent *himself* to decide out of his religious directedness toward God's will and invitation, what risks he may take or should avoid? As long as the penitent shows good faith, the priest shall trust him. Should he reach the conclusion that the penitent, more or less consciously, is deceiving himself, then he can frankly but religiously raise the question of good faith: "Do you really think that God does not ask this from you?" Or even: "Are you wholly sincere before God?" But only in a case of evident bad faith might a refusal of absolution be justified, because in that event the religious meaning of the sacrament itself is endangered.

From all that has been said it is clear that the function of psychological judgment, so risky in view of our modern realization of the inextricable blending of freedom and determinism, is being reduced to a minimum in the sacrament of the remission of sins, and that, far from endangering the religious meaning of confession, this raises it to a new level of integrity. The psychologically talented priest, even the professional priest-psychotherapist, may use all the subtle power of his empathy and his scientific skill in the confessional, provided that he uses them in the service not of a psychological but of a religious event. And one who is less talented psychologically can be a confessor inspired by grace and bestowing grace through the purity of his religious direction.

As a "holy simpleton" the Curé of Ars was far from being a psychotherapist, and from the reports jotted down about him it is evident that his advice contained nothing which was humanly profound or sensational. Nevertheless, the railroad station of Lyons had to provide a special ticket-window to sell round-trip tickets to Ars, exceptionally valid for eight days, because one generally had to wait that long before entering the confessional. There can be no other explanation than that the whole manner of this psychologically unskilled priest whose holiness made him an expert in God's ways and whose saintly life spoke louder than his words, had such connaturality with Christ's redeeming love that it was capable of penetrating all illusions and complexes to bring the very depths of a human conscience into dialog with that love.

SINFUL MAN IN THE CHURCH

1. Pastoral Work Outside the Confessional

In the confessional the priest may, to a certain extent, ignore the psychological problems of his penitent. However, when he gives *advice and direction outside the confessional* this is no longer possible. For people do not come to him only with their purely religious or moral needs; those needs are often enmeshed in wholly non-religious and even material concerns. And even when a presumed or real moral need is presented to him, all kinds of psychological obstacles or infantile images projected onto the priest often make a consciously religious solution impossible. It is true that when anyone turns in his need to a priest rather than to an organization or a physician there is always in the background some religious need consciously or unconsciously seeking satisfaction. But only by finding solutions for all the difficulties that bar and repress this deepest question in the consciousness of the person can the priestly help penetrate to the real core of the trouble and exercise its mediating function in restoring the dialog with God in faith and in love.

When asked for *information,* the priest may, of course, *teach* and explain or give practical advice. As a rule, however, such a request for information conceals an *existential* question, a moral need speaks through it. Should the priest answer as a teacher or as a spiritual director, God's word, which he intends to utter, will in fact be caught up at once in all the prejudices, affective projections, defense reactions or rationalizations of the listener and unavoidably misinterpreted. Without any intention on the part of either, the conversation turns into a dialog between two deaf people in which the longing of the penitent, listening out of the depths of his soul, cannot reach the real meaning of what the priest is trying to tell him, very sincerely perhaps, but out of his own limitations—perhaps out of a rigid scholastic book knowledge or a too restricted experience of life. The same thing is true for books on guidance in every field. The reason they are of little avail is that every reader reads them through his own glasses; all kinds of unconscious motives make him select certain elements, so that some things, possibly of secondary importance, captivate his whole attention, while other extremely important aspects, which the author may have strongly emphasized, are given no heed and vanish wholly from memory.

Furthermore, the priest is forced to make a judgment concerning the moral-religious value of the opinions and actions submitted by the visitor, and he will have to base it on a collection of symptoms proposed to him out of the uncertain, jumbled and obscure opinions of his interlocutor. Even if such a diagnosis is made with respectful, tentative empathy, the danger of mistakes is immense and their consequences often incalculable. And how easily the priest's own doubts of conscience, his pharisaical conception of justice, or personal infantilisms can make their influence felt in such judgments. Moreover, Christ's "do not judge and you will not be judged" warns us very explicitly against every cocksure judgment about the real relation of freedom and determinism in the actions of our fellow men.

The only solution lies, then, in *listening in silence* to the other. That listening must be of such a nature and intensity that it appeals to the other's deepest self, invites him to express himself from his "heart," from the deepest core of his being, and to unravel the tangled skein of his situation gradually by means of this spiritual-instinctive power of discrimination. It is a listening which gives the other the absolute certitude of being understood and accepted, the total certitude also that a harmonious growth can emerge out of his own deeper self. It is a listening that has much in common with the silent invitation of God's call to man.

This listening accomplishes much more than the doubtful judgment of an outsider concerning the actions of the person in need. It enables him to have such an authentic experience of his own freedom and of his own vocation that he himself succeeds with growing accuracy in separating the free from the unfree strands of his being. It decides nothing in his place, but it makes possible the release of a conscience caught in the grip of taboos and infantilisms, and an adult welcoming of the call of grace.

The conditions and technique for this kind of conversation have been extensively explained by experts.[10] For our purpose it will suffice to refer the reader to these works. Only a few objections which some priests present against that method may be briefly answered here.

First, the question may be raised whether such listening is not attuned to the purely *natural possibilities* of human freedom; whether it does not ignore the whole tension between grace and sin in the supernatural sense. It seems to me that such an objection is based on an artificial distinction between nature and the supernatural. In the concrete there is no such thing as man in the state of pure nature; the tension between sin and grace, God's invitation to a life of intimacy with him and the response to it in faith or unbelief, love or aversion, is always present and active in every human being. Hence it will be continually at work when that person is facing himself under the influence of the priest's listening. The very fact that the inner need looks for a solution from a priest and expresses itself in the presence of a man of God is evidence that this tension is more decisively at work than the person in question may suspect. This will often be clear from the final outcome of the meeting. On the other hand, might not an overstressed confidence in a directive intervention mean an overvaluation by the priest himself of his instrumental function within the encounter of the believer and God? True, faith comes also from hearing, and should be preached in season and out of season. But this applies to the objective preaching of the word. Its subjective acceptance in faith can be accomplished only through an immediate attraction by God, and the less we obstruct this attraction by the Father with our words and our human influences, the freer God's grace is to do its work unhindered.

Hence the answer becomes clear to another frequent objection. It goes like this: the fact of the matter is that in such conversations the person involved will quite soon center his attention almost wholly *on himself,* manifesting little or no explicit religious concern. This is a real problem, and it is an unsettled question whether a too rigid application of the technique of non-directive counseling—usually borrowed from psychotherapy—may not hinder some other functions of the priest's meeting with the disturbed or guilty person. In his ordinary pastoral work the priest's function as a mediator demands a very supple availability, and allowing himself to be caught up in specialization will generally not contribute to his effectiveness in this role. On the other hand, we must emphasize that speaking explicitly of spiritual matters is not always the most direct route to a religious encounter. *Even God can be talked to death.* What we must effect by non-directive talking is often a real change in the level of the person's value system and his whole thinking on religious matters. Words may often be an obstacle here, because talking in the religious idiom may give the person the illusion of moving on the religious plane, whereas he is clinging to the pseudo-religious. It is a remarkable fact that sometimes it is precisely at those moments when an authentic religious discovery has begun to emerge that the inner resistance expresses itself in an effort to withdraw and take refuge in familiar religious concepts. "I do not come here to learn psychology but to hear God's word from you"—that sudden reproach will more often than one thinks be an effort on the part of the counselee to flee from a real facing of God, which the listening attention of the priest is threatening to bring about. Likewise in the priest, the human satisfaction of speaking with unction and conviction about God may mean a flight from the "He must increase, I must decrease" of one who self-effacingly prepares the way of the Lord.

It is not only in individual meetings with the faithful that a non-directive attitude on the part of the priest is to be recommended. In some sectors of *collective pastoral work* too it offers great advantages. Besides the objective preaching of the glad tidings and catechetical instruction, the Christian elite is becoming increasingly aware of the need for transforming abstract doctrine, through group discussion, into something which can be lived in a personal way, for seeking together, in a collective exchange of views, solutions to the concrete problems of Christian life. The aim of the discussion leader in such groups cannot consist in being listened to, in teaching or directing in such a way as to paralyze every inquiry with his ready-made solutions, which often miss the point entirely. His presence should instead act as a catalyst, through which the whole potential of the group with respect to semi-conscious knowledge and vitally assimilated experience may emerge in full clarity and take shape in a collectively discovered acquisition. Especially where deciding one's personal position in concrete problems of conscience is concerned, this modern form of Socratic maieutics is more conducive to the development of a mature insight than an

authoritarian solution imposed from without or a finely
wrought casuistry.

All this presupposes in the priest a certain acquaintance
with the current conceptions of psychological insight and psychological techniques. May we not expect of every priest that,
without being a specialist in psychology, he will not be totally
unaware of the scientific laws of that psychic life on which
his profession so often forces him to exert a decisive influence?

2. Holiness and Complexes

The renewed insight into the relation between freedom and
determinism in man not only has a strong bearing upon
practical pastoral work, it may also force us, on the theoretical
plane, to revise our whole concept of Christian perfection
and holiness. Besides the centuries-old problem of freedom
and grace, the complementary problem of the relation between *grace and determinism* is steadily receiving more attention. To what extent does holiness depend on psychic factors?
Is there such a thing as a neurotic sanctity?[11]

The question is not a simple one, and perhaps we should
begin by demythologizing the word *holiness* itself to some
extent. In Scripture the term saint is synonymous with the
Christian living in grace, the *living member* of Christ. Very
early, however, the concept of holiness became attached to
the idea of an *extraordinary growth* in grace, the total donation of a concrete human existence in response to God's
invitation to love. The original type of that perfect self-
donation was Mary. As the Church started to acknowledge
the holiness of some individuals publicly and to present them
for the veneration of the faithful, the word spontaneously
acquired an even narrower meaning in the minds of many
people. For them holiness became synonymous with the like-

lihood of being canonized. However, belonging to God in perfection of grace is not the only norm for canonization. Only that form of holiness is *canonizable* in which grace has so flowered in the life and conduct of a Christian as to be productive of such heroic selflessness and love for others, such a superhuman inner equilibrium and harmony of the total personality, that in this person the conformity with Christ assumes, as it were, a concrete form and raises up his whole existence as a diaphanous sign of God for all men. Such a holiness, therefore, supposes not only a total self-donation in response to God's call but also a very special vocation; it is some kind of moral miracle presented by God to the Church at a certain time and in a certain situation, one of which a human being is the predestined instrument.

The best spiritual authors always keep in mind the twofold meaning of the word holiness. But in ordinary preaching this was not always done, and the answer to the question, "Is everybody called to holiness?" frequently remained very ambiguous. It was often made to seem as if only our lack of generosity prevented all of us from becoming canonizable saints. At any rate, the outwardly perceptible result, the so-called *exercise of heroic virtue,* became as a matter of course the accepted criterion for the inner self-donation to God. And under the influence of an unconscious Pelagianism (which continued to proliferate in the Church), perfection often became a ready-made form, an abstract blueprint which one was supposed to reproduce to the best of one's ability in one's own life, and whose ideal pattern could be approached more or less by everyone. This abstract perfection, some kind of greatest common denominator of canonized sanctity, invited Christians to a purely material imitation—we might almost say, to an aping—of the lives of the saints. And in this imita-

tion one's own ascetic endeavor obviously had to receive
much more emphasis than grace, which was considered available as a matter of course. That grace, moreover, was seen in
terms not so much of a personal dialog as of a force of pro-
pulsion, moving us towards the pre-ordained abstract ideal.

Possibly the discovery of the considerable degree of determinism in man's activity has dealt the death blow to that
unconscious Pelagianism. We are forced to distinguish again
very carefully the several meanings of the word "holiness,"
and we can no longer take the very special vocation of the
canonized saint as a norm of evaluation for the average
Christian—not to mention equating holiness naturalistically
with a superior, and perhaps fortuitous, human equilibrium.

If holiness is nothing but the fullness of the free self-
donation of a concrete existence to God's love of predilection,
it cannot depend on what is psychically determined, but only
on the free response of man's will to grace. And we have no
evidence that the perfection of that response must necessarily
take shape in a complete integration of the psychic elements,
within the harmony of grace, in a beautifully human maturity.
True, the self-donation to grace may likewise have that effect,
and graphological analysis of the personalities of quite a
number of canonized saints shows that psychologically they
gave little indication of being cut out for their vocation. But
who is to say that grace cannot equally well find a perfect
response within a never totally conquered illness, and within
the helplessness of a handicapped, neurotic, incurably unbal-
anced person? One might even wonder whether that holiness
of humble acquiescence hoping against hope, of resigned
submission in unflagging love to a life of falling and rising,
to the painful helplessness of an ascent constantly slowed
down by hereditary defects, mistakes in education, or over-

whelming circumstances, may not often mean a greater victory of divine grace, hence a really greater holiness, than the unhindered growth of a more spontaneously balanced soul or of one more favored by nature.

3. Determinism and Original Sin

Finally, the discoveries of psychology and sociology can help us considerably in giving new meaning to the notions of *solidarity* in evil and collective responsibility, and in attuning theological thought to a clearer conception of that more than individual dimension attributed to sin by Holy Scripture which Christian faith has termed *"original sin."*[12] Even before the child can consciously experience his freedom, he is profoundly influenced, often marked for life, by a world and a community, and by all the greed, the cupidity, the pride, the divisions, quarrels and jealousies, the inherited handicaps and the moral corruption which exist in that world and in that community. By far the greatest proportion of the suffering, the isolation and the despair which a man ever has to undergo —the greatest part especially of all that makes him immature and defenseless before life's blows—comes from the evil and the insufficiencies which have been brought to bear on him through his education, his environment and all his contemporaries. Likewise he himself, in his turn, will directly or indirectly spoil life's happiness for others by the darkness and evil in his own soul. Thus also his parents, educators and contemporaries carried within their own beings the shadows of former generations and the burden of a long human inheritance. Modern man is keenly aware of the inevitability, and at the same time of the unnaturalness, of that evil as it manifests itself in each person. Not without reason has it been said that the picture of man's psychic depths as presented to us

by modern art and the modern novel is one of an absurd in-
humanity on his part, some kind of original sin without
redemption.[13]

It is a striking fact that Catholic dogmatic theology is
becoming more and more inclined to conceive original sin as
a *situation* brought about in mankind from the very beginning,
an initial option which keeps spreading more widely as mankind expands and growing stronger with the individual sins
of each person. On the other hand, each man, even before he
is able to use his freedom, is by the very fact of being historically situated within mankind unavoidably caught up in the
sphere of influence of that evil, as in an area of darkness
which he cannot conquer by his own power and which holds
him back from the meeting with God. Men have first become
fully aware of this general situation of sinfulness in their
rejection of Christ. At the same time, they have realized that
only the new man Christ can free us from that situation, by
making us in him into a "new creature" born of God, so that,
however strongly we may continue to be held in this world of
sinfulness, in a solidarity devoid of freedom, we may nevertheless receive the power, through and in him, of "becoming
children of God" by our free response to God's love.

Thus the full implications of psychic determinism would
ultimately have to be referred to the "mystery of iniquity,"
and it would no longer appear to be a merely natural factor.
On the other hand, in this view original sin would not be
some kind of juridical imputation of a past event, but a situation which continues to exert its effects, and to be accepted
and confirmed by every personal sin.

3

Legal Ethics
or Situation Ethics?

The deep change in the moral consciousness of Christians concealed under the label "situation ethics" is a climate rather than a doctrine, a kind of spiritual groping rather than a fully formed theory. True, with the support of all kinds of theories and opinions an attempt is being made at systematization; nevertheless the phenomenon is first and foremost the result of an alteration in modern man's feeling and thinking, the repercussion on the moral sense of a picture of the world and of man in the midst of a crisis of growth.

Two factors especially, working in opposite directions, have influenced this process: On the one hand, the *decrease* of the *social protection* of conscience; on the other hand, the *increase* of *social pressure* upon it.

The self-discovery experienced by man during the past century has given rise in him to the urgent need for a *mature autonomy* in his existence, for a freedom from all bonds of dependence. There is a general feeling that for the first time in history man is being offered the chance of becoming fully himself. For the first time he sees almost unlimited possibilities for ridding himself of the domination of things by means of his technical mastery over nature. The abolition of man's enslavement to his fellow men seems also to be within his immediate reach. The struggle for emancipation of the proletariat, decolonization, racial integration, the very rapid economic and social emergence of the newer nations, the fight against every form of paternalism—all are symptoms of a mystique of man which is breaking through irresistibly. Many feel that the breaking of every bond with religious authority is an indispensable factor in this process of self-emancipation, while those who remain believers, swept along by this fresh surge of vitality, are endeavoring to clarify their religious attitude and make it more authentic, to rid their church membership of all paternalistic traditions.

All this has entailed the *disintegration* of quite a number of social structures which held man in bonds but which at the same time afforded him protection against the immaturity of his own conscience. Within a few decades, closed rural communities have been thrown open to the most diverse influences and opinions; marriage has evolved from a socially conditioned pairing to a spontaneous meeting of love. We might further mention the passage from a closed to an open family, from a sheltering to a venturesome education; the growing awareness of philosophic pluralism within the community; the shift from an overorganized collective apostolate to a personal search for Christian authenticity on the part of individuals or small groups. This new climate confronts the individual with much more frequent and more difficult personal decisions. He is no longer allowed to follow the path beaten by the herd; he must, and he wants to, seek his own path at his own risk.

This heightened awareness of autonomous responsibility, growing towards maturity, is enhanced by the *threat* arising from the complexity of modern life and the danger of robotization and *depersonalization* which the present social setup involves. All that has been said about this in the previous chapter appears to modern man as an unavoidable toll for his progress and likewise as totally opposed to his will for freedom; he tolerates the external bonds with resignation, without allowing his inner free decisions to be affected by that process of enslavement.

It is a universal phenomenon that modern, and especially Western, man is firmly set against all constraint of his personal moral decisions on the part of any outside agency whatsoever —by the remnants of outmoded social institutions, by ideologies or traditions, by the new forms of pressure, by modern social structures or patterns of thought. Before the sanctuary of his personal decision of conscience every influence from without must come to a halt: *only* his *inner freedom* decides what is good and what is evil.

THE PROBLEM

This new moral feeling spontaneously looks for support in certain theories and trends of thought in which resistance to traditional morality has taken shape.

A critique of this kind has been presented from three very different points of view, and all three have had a great influence upon the development of a "new morality" even within Catholic circles.

THE "DOUBLE MORALITY"

The first direction is that of double morality. Here the ethics of law and the ethics of creative freedom are not only put side by side but are diametrically opposed to each other as two irreducible forms of morality. The former is considered

as unauthentic, the latter as the only authentic and valid form
of morality.

1. Bergson and "Les deux sources"

Before the Second World War Henri Bergson[14] had sharply
drawn the distinction between the two sources of ethical activity, which were, in his opinion, wholly heterogeneous. He had
related that distinction to his theory of the evolution of creation. The title of his book, *Les deux sources de la morale et
de la religion,* emphasized the contrast between the two
sources, and in his work he observes that the two forms may
influence each other and appear to blend, but that these so-
called blended forms are in fact nothing but the relatively
peaceful coexistence of two essentially and radically irreconcilable life attitudes.

The creative surge of evolution, the *"élan vital,"* as Bergson
calls it, leaves in its path a series of ossified remnants from
which that creative *élan* has departed and which, in the form
of closed groups or communities, aim only at self-preservation.
The primitive human communities of which all our present
social forms are mere superstructures are thus an ossification,
a fixation, of the *élan vital.* Hence the drive for self-preservation will be felt by the individual as a powerful social pressure; not, however, as in animals, under the form of mere
instinct, but, since man is endowed with an intellect, under
the form of a spiritual yet quasi-instinctive urge for adaptation and conformity. This *urge* for self-preservation of the
group, *introjected* in the individual as a spiritual instinct, is
"obligation" (*l'obligation morale*) and constitutes the basis of
what Bergson calls "closed morality" (*morale close*). On the
other hand, the original *élan* always continues to operate in

some privileged individuals, each one of whom constitutes a
new species of human being. In them it takes the form of a
creative spiritual "emotion," leading to a universal human
morality no longer bound to the group, a *"morale ouverte"*
which, for the time being, is finding its peak in Christian
ethics. It is obvious that in his opinion the *"morale close"* is
an inferior, even an unauthentic form of morality, and that
only the creative freedom of the *élan vital* is capable of estab-
lishing an authentic, universal human morality.

2. Hesnard and "Morality without Sin"

An even stronger influence proceeded from the works of
A. *Hesnard*, chairman of the Société psychanalytique de
France, not only because, starting from the data of Freudian
psychoanalysis, he appealed more directly to the readers' own
experience, but more particularly because in his second work,
Morale sans péché, he converted the considerations previously
set forth in his *L'univers morbide de la faute* into an all-out
attack upon traditional Catholic morality.

The child, so he says—and also mankind in its primitive
forms—necessarily passes through a stage of mere *taboo morality* in which unruly instinctivity is held in check only by
the threatening pressure of an external authority or of an
inhibiting superego. At that age the *feeling of guilt* is not yet
a real judgment of conscience; it is pre-ethical, instinctive and
magical. Authentic morality exists only where the blind infantile guilt feeling for the "fault" or "transgression" has yielded
to the responsible, fully conscious self-donation in love to
one's work for one's fellow men. When in a physically adult
person conscience remains strongly influenced and hindered
by the guilt-morality of the infantile psyche, we have an

infantile, hence a neurotic, conscience; we are entering the
"morbid universe of the fault," where morality is equated
with taboo.

Although the Gospels open some vistas of really adult
morality, based upon love of one's fellow man, Hesnard continues, very soon education in the Church and in Christian
families, presenting itself in the guise of religious precepts
and in gospel terminology, has effected a return to a morality
of "transgression," thus greatly hindering the growth of Western mankind towards an adult morality. Taking morality out
of its living context in the concrete activity of man within his
community, that education has sought a norm for moral action
in a reality which is alien to man in the concrete, a "divine
law," thus barring him from a personal moral commitment
and driving him back, in fact, into a taboo morality. Moreover
it has strengthened the baneful, neuroticizing influence of
that taboo morality by shifting the grounds of the taboo from
external transgression to *inner guilt*, to "sin." It teaches man
to experience the mere desire of the wrong action as something forbidden, as a taboo. Thus every instinctive impulse
leads to guilt feelings, to some kind of "preventive contrition"
for the possible transgression, and man is impelled to extend
his control of his deepest drives to their very roots, to try to
neutralize them as far as possible. The more he engages in
this effort, the more keenly he experiences the fact that these
drives are inextricably linked with his very existence. This
morality of inner "sin," therefore, leads to a kind of *"culpabilité d'existence"* (existential guilt), a feeling of guilt which
embraces one's whole existence and is rendered more acute
by the idea of the "stain of original sin." All this is a tremen-
dous hindrance to real morality. First because this hopeless
struggle so absorbs man's psychic forces as to make him

unable to meet his fellow man in real love. Next because the rejected instinctivity reacts with a vengeance, bringing about all kinds of harmful effects: in the individual, a tyrannical convention-morality which judges others harshly and intolerantly and makes them pay very dearly for sins "one does not commit"; in the group, the fostering, in the name of abstract principles and ideals (truth, fatherland, freedom, justice, and so on) of things which in private life one would consider indecent and prohibited—vengeance, oppression, murder, and war.

Moreover, the great non-Catholic systems of morality are not much better off in Hesnard's view, because in the final analysis they only laicize Christian morality, replace the divine law by some other abstract conceptual system which always remains alien to concrete human experience: the categorical imperative of Kant, the abstract idea of the community in the school of Durkheim, the future ideal of a classless society in communistic morality. They all sacrifice real man to a myth, thus degenerating to the level of *"mytho-morality."*

On the other hand, for the situation ethics he defends "there would be only one evil: real evil, committed from person to person. There would be only one good: the action performed for the other person and with the other person. That morality would have only *one object,* which would constitute the only moral reality: the ever more perfect *relation between person and person:* collaboration, fellowship, tolerance, mutual assistance, love and liberality—devotion not to an abstract idea, but to man."[15]

3. Existentialistic Ethics

The opposition between law and freedom is pushed to the extreme in the atheistic forms of existentialism. Although in their whole spirit they are utterly opposed to the Christian way of thinking, they too, through the discussions to which they gave rise, have exerted an undeniable influence on the crisis in Catholic ethics. The most radical assertion of the unauthenticity of every objective norm and of the *absolute superiority* of *subjective freedom* has been made by *Jean-Paul Sartre* and by *Simone de Beauvoir*.[16]

The values which inspire man's activity are not preordained, either by a divine ideal or one standing absolutely outside man, or by a "nature" pre-existing as an objective datum. As soon as one yields to objectivity of this kind, one is plunged into "bad faith." Man can be of good faith only through the unconditional welcoming of his free and responsible subjectivity. Values are created only and exclusively by man's *freedom*, by his *creative arbitrariness*, as it expresses itself within the situation. To be responsible for oneself and for the others does not mean, for Sartre, to have to render an account to them or to an abstract ideal of oneself, but freely to assume the inherent risks of being creatively free. "There is nothing left in heaven, neither good nor evil, nor anybody to give me order. For I am a human being, Jupiter, and every human being must invent his way." That remark of Orestes in *Les Mouches* very well expresses how only man's freedom can be a norm and a scale of values for itself. Nothing has any value, except through the place it assumes in my plans. Important means: important for me. I am fated to be free "of" every coercion; what I am free "for" can only be decided by my freedom, as it shapes my relations to things and to people within the situation.

With other existentialists the unbridled arbitrariness of Sartrian freedom is to some extent held in check. For instance, Fr. *Jeanson*, who feels that the conscious subject would negate himself if he engaged in conflict with his own freedom; that is, if he failed to remain steady and faithful to the once elected project by becoming incoherent with his own choice; or again, if the subject's freedom should turn against the freedom of others, thus ignoring the fact that he is intersubjectively conditioned. *G. Gusdorf* goes even further when he acknowledges that there are fundamental values in the identical situation of all human beings whose totality constitutes the "human condition."[17]

"EVOLUTIONARY" MORALITY

The second direction which the critique of morality has taken views *classical,* so-called "objective," morality as inextricably bound up with a *static* image of man, an immutable essence from which eternally valid norms might be deduced termed the "natural law." The *dynamic image* of a human being in a steady process of evolution presented to us by modern science would demand an *evolving* morality as well. The norm of man's activity might still be situated in his "human nature," but that concept would not mean a fixed datum, but rather a goal to be reached and a prospect to be realized. Man can become himself only by becoming other than he is. In other words, we should seek our concept of human nature more in the future than in the past, and a morality which became conservative—that is static—would *ipso facto* cease to correspond to the natural law.

This evolutionary conception of morality has been accepted by *atheistic humanism,* especially by a certain number of members of the International Humanistic Association. In the convention held at Amsterdam in 1952 its guiding principle was formulated by Julian Huxley as follows: "Human destiny

must be looked at not *sub specie aeternitatis,* but *sub specie
evolutionis.*" Applied to the concept of morality this means
that human morality is based on an idea of value that is not
a creation of personal arbitrariness but something suprapersonal which yet does not come from outside man. This
conception of value evolves in mankind; hence it depends, in
its application, on collective feeling, common insight and the
culture of the time. Of its very nature no value is wholly
above challenge, for every one may become problematic at
some stage of the process of evolution.[18]

The vast majority of present-day adherents of an evolutionary morality adopt the *vision of Teilhard de Chardin,* whose
concept of each individual's and each generation's contribu-
tion to the construction and completion of the noosphere
indeed looks for a norm of morality in becoming rather than
in being. It is to be noted that by identifying the ultimate
center of noogenesis—point Omega—with Christ, Teilhard
makes that evolutionary morality coincide with the fulfillment
of mankind's religious vocation. Therefore, when he demands
that we look towards the future, he appeals very specially to
the Catholic moralist, and his vision has had a profound
influence on the efforts at renewal of Catholic ethics.[19]

THE OPPOSITION BETWEEN LAW AND
GRACE IN PROTESTANTISM

Finally, a third direction derives not from the Catholic
thesis of grace building on nature, but from a specifically
Protestant conception of the dialectical opposition between
nature and grace. Yet this conception too has exerted an
undeniable influence upon Catholic situation ethics. The most

outspoken proponent of the relativizing of natural morality by God's grace was *Kierkegaard*.[20]

As opposed to natural thinking, faith appears to him as that which is humanly absurd, wherein one must dare to make the leap of unconditional trust in a personal donation to God which no human guarantee can justify. It follows that in this relationship, natural moral activity is transcended and rendered relative; it belongs to the world of sin which is condemned and rendered worthless by grace. The law cannot be a norm for the dialog with God; that dialog stands by itself and is the norm for all the rest. The individual character of *God's call* or invitation is a norm for itself and triumphs over the generality of the moral law. In his *Fear and Trembling* Kierkegaard describes the immolation of Isaac which God asked of Abraham as the prototype of the triumph of the religiously absurd over the rationality of the moral level. He found the same conflict also in his own life when he gave up marriage with his beloved Regina Olsen whom he, like another Abraham, felt he had to offer on the altar of his personal vocation.

Kierkegaard's thesis has exerted a great influence on Protestant situation ethics (Thielicke, Brunner, Althaus, Wunsch, etc.) which, although not always so radically denying the validity of the moral law, nevertheless constantly subordinates it to the personal dialog in grace of God with the human being.

SITUATION ETHICS WITHIN CATHOLICISM

All the trends and influences we have described have affected Catholic thinking also and have converged in a strong, widespread tendency towards a *Catholic situation ethics.*

It is not easy to cite specific names of Catholic authors in this connection. Most Catholic theologians who have written on the subject have simply presented a *critical judgment* on situation ethics and warned against exaggerations. In 1950 K. Rahner already took a clear position; he was followed by many others. In 1952 Pius XII came out against situation ethics several times. In 1956 the *Holy Office* made public a note to the same effect.[21] More than against specific authors, all these warnings were aimed at a mentality very widespread among the faithful as well as among moralists. As this mentality had no precise writings and explanations to depend on, it showed a propensity for emotional reactions, mingling justified criticism with reckless approval of positions which could not be reconciled with Catholic thinking.

One of the primary forms that mentality takes is an almost universal, but all too well justified, *discontent* with the usual *textbook morality*. It is charged that this morality is negatively protective, fostering infantilism instead of stimulating adult self-reliance; that it depersonalizes the human situation of the individual into abstract casuistry; that it fragments the organic growth to a Christian fullness of life into a multiplicity of legalistic precepts and prohibitions, worked out into the minutest detail with hairsplitting rabbinism; that, under the influence of an outmoded form of spirituality, it distorts the unity of body and soul in man into an opposition, and attempts to freeze the evolving picture of man in a static notion of nature; that in fact it separates ethics from religion and chokes off the autonomous decision of conscience under a divine authority nominalistically conceived in a merely heteronomous way.

That discontent leads to *practical positions* deviating sharply

from the usual casuistry for definite problems which the
Christian conscience faces so often in these confused, rapidly
evolving times. The Pope himself mentions specific questions
to which situation ethics is often applied by Catholics: giving
up one's faith out of alleged spiritual honesty; contraceptive
practices in marriage; sexual relations between those who are
engaged; divorce; differences of opinion with ecclesiastical
authorities (e.g. among the "progressive priests" in the countries behind the iron curtain).[22] It is not difficult to add to
these another long series of problems which have received
much attention of late: preventive suicide on the part of
soldiers or secret agents, the abortion of raped women or the
so-called "ethical" abortion; euthanasia and the killing of
"monsters" or of badly deformed children; fertilization *in vitro*
or the artificial development of a foetus; the marriage of
priests who have given up their function, and so on. Widely
discussed cases mentioned in *novels* make some of these problems into topics of public conversation.

In a more theoretical and *generalizing* form that mentality
springs up today in popular *slogans*: "What do the priests
know about all this?" ". . . . as long as you honestly follow
your conscience . . . ." "I'll decide that for myself." In the
private discussions of confessors and moralists too one often
meets the tendency to transpose onto the totality of the ethical
law, principles which govern the application of positive laws
(there is no obligation when it becomes too inconvenient,
etc.). One starts from the unstated premise that something
which is very difficult loses its obligatory character when existentially it is no longer felt to be feasible or acceptable.
Whereas classical moral doctrine appealed only to the determining influences of a psychological or social nature for these

cases with a view to questioning the presence of "full knowledge and free consent," many moralists nowadays seem to cast the objective obligation itself into doubt.

How does this situation ethics of Catholic inspiration stand *theoretically* with respect to the law? If we try to reduce the prevailing opinions to some sort of greatest common denominator, we might say that the value of the general norms is not simply denied but, in the phrase of Pius XII, "shifted from the center to the periphery."[23]

Here is the way the note of the Holy Office tries to summarize the assertions of situation ethics of which it disapproves:

"The adherents of this system feel that the last and *decisive norm* of human action does not lie in an objective system of values determined by the natural law and known with certainty from it, but in an *inner light* and judgment of the individual spirit, whereby the latter realizes what he has to do in the concrete situation. Hence the ultimate decision of conscience in man does not, in their opinion, derive from the application of a general law to a particular case, taking prudentially into account the circumstances of the situation (such is the traditional teaching of objective morality defended by the great authors), but from that inner light and judgment. The objective validity and exactness of such a judgment will, at least in many instances, not find its final *norm*, nor even have to find its final norm, *in any objective* standard, independent of man's subjective evaluation. That judgment will be sufficient unto itself."

According to the same authors, the *traditional* notion of *"natural law" no longer satisfies;* one must appeal to the notion of *"existing nature,"* which generally represents no absolute and objective value, but only a relative, hence a *changeable value*, with the possible exception of a few data and principles referring to "metaphysical" (that is, absolute and unchangeable) human nature. The traditional notion of "natural law" stands on the level of this merely relative value. Much of what is, at present, considered as an absolute postulate of the natural law is based—again, according to the opinions and the doctrine of these authors—only on the notion of "existing nature." Hence it possesses only a relative and changeable value and must be adapted to the ever changing situations.[24]

ELEMENTS OF A SOLUTION

Taking into consideration both the warnings of ecclesiastical authority and the valuable elements contained in the new trends, the question must now be asked and answered: What is the value, what are the limits of the law, and what is, for the Christian conscience, the relation of freedom to the law?[25]

VALUE AND LIMITS OF THE LAW

In order to understand the relation between love, freedom and law, it seems necessary to keep before one's eyes the *different levels*, mentioned in our first chapter, on which these words can be understood. This has been too frequently overlooked both by those who appeal to the law and by those who oppose the law in the name of "love" and "freedom."

1. Natural Law and Positive Law on the Moral Level

It is true that on the level of *instinct*—that is, as long as the law is experienced as a coercion merely imposed from without —mature freedom and external law confront each other as *irreconcilable* elements without anything in common. It is only on the *moral* level that the question of the relation between law and freedom takes on a meaning—at least, if the concept of law keeps a meaning acceptable on that level. What might that meaning be?

For a philosophy inspired by Christianity freedom cannot be reduced to a mere creative arbitrariness. This philosophy conceives man's deepest nature as a relation to God; the fact of being a creature, of existing by and in relation to Another, must affect man's whole unfolding self-realization. Although human freedom does indeed really create value out of itself, it is never only a freedom "from" every coercion, but is always also a freedom "towards" an intended fullness of possible self-realization. That fullness is not prefigured as an abstract scheme, a blueprint to be reproduced, but as a *dynamically inviting possibility,* a concrete project to be carried out in the midst of a concrete situation in which man's "self" presents its demands to an "ego" consciously realizing itself. "Become what thou art" is, on the moral level, the fundamental law by which the authenticity or unauthenticity of a human development, and of the separate actions in which that development takes shape, can be measured.

That inner law of growth has traditionally borne the name "natural law." Hence in its classical meaning the term "natural law" has no connection with the physical or biological concept of "nature," formerly in frequent use in the positive sciences and in ethics, with which it is often wrongly identified even nowadays (for instance, in the treatment of sexual problems). Thus some actions are supposed to be "according to" or "against" nature. But an action which is biologically "according to" nature may very well be morally in conflict with the "natural law." Hence the fact that the notion of "nature" is outmoded in the positive sciences cannot be used as an argument against the natural law in the moral sense, since it has no connection whatsoever with it.

Nor is the natural law in its classical meaning the collection of abstract principles or formulations to which textbook morality has often reduced it, under the influence of the seventeenth- and eighteenth-century theories of natural right. Historically the appeal to the natural law has arisen precisely from the resistance of personal conscience to the arbitrariness of written laws; it appealed to an *unwritten law,* an inborn knowledge of what man ought to do and ought not to do in order to be and to become authentically himself. Among the great classical authors that meaning of the natural law has been maintained in all its integrity.

Thus we find, for example, in Thomas Aquinas the following description: "The rational creature is subject in a more perfect manner than the others to divine providence, insofar namely as it shares this providence and becomes providence for itself and for others. Hence it shares the eternal law and possesses a natural inclination towards its authentic act and finality. It is precisely this sharing of the eternal law in the rational creature which is called natural law."[26]

Hence in its original meaning the natural law is a *dynamic existing reality,* an ordering of man towards his self-perfection and his self-realization, through all the concrete situations of his life and in intersubjective dialog with his fellow man and with God. Although for us the expression may have too static a resonance, the reality it embraces can be integrated without any difficulty in a dynamic picture of the world and still keep its full meaning. For it is precisely man's becoming which is prefigured in it. The norm of man's action is not so much what he is as what he is to become.

The dynamic character of the natural law does *not in the least* mean a variability in that law in the sense that it might be *arbitrarily modified* under the influence of individual or collective feeling. It is precisely the law of evolution, as it appears, for instance, in Teilhard's vision, that an increasing complexity of structures goes along with an increasing interiorization of consciousness, and that this development does not proceed in a steady way but shows, at definite thresholds, sudden total modifications of aspect, situation or disposition.

Besides wholly new phenomena, running in the line of evolution, *regressions too* and ossifications may occur, which can be judged as such and distinguished from the progressive phenomena only by referring them to the general law of development. It is possible that in evolving humanity some implications of the natural law may rise to full consciousness only gradually, or that moral intuition in its full purity may detach itself only in a very gradual way from certain representations or projections in which it was caught. It is even possible that, on reaching certain thresholds, the growing moral awareness may show wholly new aspects and forms. Yet not every subjective modification in the moral sentiments of individuals or of groups lies in the line of authentic evolution. And it is precisely the awareness of what developing man ought to become, hence the inner and dynamic natural law, which *allows* us to *distinguish* authentic developments from regressions and decay.[27]

Thus it is possible that reverence for life may demand certain things which formerly did not emerge so clearly into consciousness. To mention only one example, we may begin to feel that the death penalty is in conflict with our growing reverence for man, hence that it is immoral. But it is impossible that mankind should authentically evolve in the direction

of a morality which would destroy or weaken the reverence
for life. Again, it is a fact that married love has only in a
very gradual manner manifested the fullness of its demands
in the mind and conscience of man. It is possible that our
insight into the structure of sexuality is still very imperfect
and that a growing awareness may, in the future, demand
much more from the authentic experience of sexual love. But
it is not possible that man should authentically evolve towards
a morality of free love, because that would go against the
grain of a humanity which is developing towards an ever
more intensive amorization.

In the final analysis the natural law does not find its norm
in the actual sentiments of humanity, but that very law
constitutes *the norm of authenticity* of the evolving sentiments
of humanity.

In a human community the natural law should not only be
active as a norm deep within every human soul. It must be
made *communicable,* available as a principle of education
and of community organization. For that purpose it must be
laid down in *fixed formulas* and coined into generally valid
rules of conduct and even into detailed applications. As soon,
however, as it is channelled into maxims and formulas, the
lifelikeness of the inner natural law and its organic connection
with the situation becomes ossified into an abstraction. It
turns into a prescription, a recipe, and it loses all contact with
ever changing reality. It must inevitably express itself in the
language of a determined cultural milieu, in the concepts of
a determined sphere of thought; often it will be interpreted
out of very limited philosophical insight. As a result, all these
formulations at once acquire a certain *coefficient of relativity.*

Yet this too does not mean that the natural law is arbitrarily
changeable. It is precisely the dynamic authenticity of the

inner natural law which serves as norm for every change in its expression. It is forever in a process of purification from all the images in which a certain time or a certain culture threaten to imprison it, expressing its changeless authenticity in the language and conceptual forms of a new time, a new culture, a new attitude towards life.

The more the basic finality towards human self-realization tries to translate itself into the *small decisions* of life, the greater the extent to which it becomes contaminated by all kinds of factors bound to that particular time; the wider, too, the *margin of imperfection* in its formulation and the greater the danger of misunderstanding and faulty interpretation. This was already fully acknowledged by classical moral doctrine and expressed, for instance, by Aquinas in the famous distinction between primary and secondary prescriptions of the natural law, where he remarks that in the practical judgment the danger of error increases as one goes down into more detailed applications *"quanto magis ad propria descenditur, tanto magis invenitur defectus"* ("the more we descend to particulars, the more we encounter defects").[23]

The *ten commandments* are mainly a practical formulation of a number of basic assertions of the natural law. A simple comparison, however, between the original formulation, as presented in Exodus (20. 1–17), with some modern catechism formulations shows to what extent, in the course of the history of salvation, the formulas have been detached from all kinds of primitive religious conceptions and antiquated social structures. And it is quite evident that this purification continues, as shown by the whole evolution of the Christian attitude towards abuses of the Holy Name, and from the often painful casuistry into which a formula such as "thou shalt not lie" has led the conceptualistic philosophy of "truth" of textbook teaching.

Not all concrete decisions in minor matters can find their norm in the natural law in such a way that only one manner of acting, one manner of tackling a certain situation, is possible. Frequently there are several ways to reach a certain end. But in a community these differences in conduct between individuals, even though each is good in itself and in accordance with the natural law, can become very harmful to the common good. Hence the need for authority to make a choice within that community between these several possibilities and to impose one of them in the form of a law universally valid for the community.

Such a law, by its very definition, is not self-evident. It is established only by the will of the legislator. That is why we call it a *positive law*. Its necessity does not derive from what it prescribes, but from the need for harmonizing the spontaneous decisions of individuals with the general welfare. Hence the positive law is a real restriction of man's free activity, but a restriction which ultimately promotes and serves that freedom.

That law too—although it unavoidably involves a certain amount of arbitrariness—is *not merely arbitrary*. It should be dictated to the legislator by his concern for the general welfare, while respecting the legitimate freedom of individual conscience.

Such a law is *by definition changeable* since it is to a great extent determined by the concrete, changing demands of a situation. It allows of exceptions in the form of dispensations foreseen by authority itself or of motives which excuse the subject from obeying it. Even while authority continues to uphold it, it may wholly lose its obligatory character because most evidently it no longer corresponds to the given situation and is injurious to the common welfare; or it is an attempt to promote the common welfare at the cost of a manifestly unreasonable and useless limitation of individual freedom; or even because it conflicts with the absolute demands of the natural law.

The virtue which maintains the superiority of the unwritten inner natural law within the application of the positive law has since time immemorial been called *"epikeia"* (*aequitas*), the virtue of equity. Under the influence of Suarez that notion, too, came to be conceived so narrowly that it was reduced to the idea of an objective *principle of interpretation* of the law, some kind of intra-legal correction of the imperfection or rigidity of the written text of the law. However, according to the conception of classical antiquity, taken over by medieval theology and based on religious principles, *epikeia* was infinitely more: it was a real virtue, hence a *disposition of the soul,* a noble inclination of the heart; it was the decision always to make the juridical serve justice, to keep the law in the service of conscience; and wherever required, to give unconditional priority to the eternal law of nature written in man's heart over every positive text of the law. It is an encouraging fact that present-day moral theology is going back to the original meaning of the word.[29]

2. The Christian Law of Life and
Laws of the Church

All that has been said up to now applies to the moral level. But the Christian lives on a religious-ethical level, and the question must be asked to what extent the meaning of the law is maintained or superseded on that level.

In our first chapter we said that the religious-ethical level is characterized by the fact that it no longer lies within the range of the development of one's own being, but depends entirely on a new, creative communication of God, inviting

man to a dialog of love whose intimacy is outside the sphere
of human initiative. Hence that invitation can be accepted
by man only if it creatively infuses in him the power to
respond to it. For "who among men knows the things of man
save the spirit of a man which is in him? Even so, the things
of God no one knows but the Spirit of God." (1 Cor. 2.11)
When, therefore, we are admitted to intimacy with God, this
is possible only because "we have received not the spirit of
the world, but the spirit that is from God, that we may know
the things that have been given us by God" (1 Cor. 2.12).

It is for this reason that we term "infused" the divine
virtues of faith, hope and charity which God's spirit evokes
in us, through which we listen to God's word with a new
power of hearing in this wholly new supernatural manner;
through which we advance towards him in a new way and
meet his love with a new heart. As in the natural trend of our
being towards its own self-development an objective law of
growth is expressed and described, this supernatural shaping
of our course through faith, hope and love will develop some
kind of *natural law of the supernatural,* an inner *law of growth
of the Holy Spirit,* imprinted in us by his influence and by
his call to us. We really are, as St. Paul says, "a letter of
Christ, composed by us, written not with ink but with the
Spirit of the living God, not on tablets of stone but on fleshly
tablets of the heart" (2 Cor. 3.3). The norm for Christian life
is no longer mere human self-development but "the charity
of God poured forth in our hearts by the Holy Spirit who has
been given to us" (Rom. 5.5; 8.11).

What is the relation between this inner law of grace and
the moral law of nature? The former does not supersede the
latter but *raises* and *completes* it. Our self-development on
the natural plane becomes a task and a vocation through

God's loving invitation; it becomes the topic of conversation
in our dialog of love with him. Because they have been taken
up into the finality of faith, hope and love, all the moral
virtues acquire a dimension of grace; they share the divine,
"infused" nature of the theological virtues.

This, however, involves a threat to the natural law much
more grave than any posed by the imperfections and weaknesses in us which are merely human. For God's grace not
only opens hitherto unsuspected prospects to our existence.
It also reveals to us the depth of our dereliction, the fact that
we are held in an unavoidable solidarity with sinful mankind,
and that we cannot escape from this bondage through our
natural powers; only grace can deliver us. The natural law
as well is assumed within the tension wrought in us by the
opposing forces of grace and sin, original sin and the redemption, concupiscence and the urgings of the spirit.

A comparison of the law of grace briefly described here
with the interpretation offered by *Hesnard* of the morality of
the Christian religion not only shows clearly that he has not
the slightest inkling of the authentic Christian awareness of
sin, it also discloses the true bearing of the *a priori* assumption which he regards as obvious, and from which his misrep-
resentation follows of necessity: his rejection of all transcend-
ence which is not that of the group over the individual and
of all experience outside the ambit of perception on a merely
psychological level. Whatever stands outside of, or higher
than, this is lumped together under the term "myth" and
rejected in its totality. Hence he sees the choice between an
infantile taboo-attitude and a morality of concrete action of
merely social inspiration as a *dilemma*. It does not so much
as dawn on him that there might be a *third possibility*: man's
ordination towards the infinite love of a God who leans over

him, inviting him. In his world closed to the sacred, in which only the profane is real, there is no room for that deepest morality of love, and he can only caricature that loving invitation into some kind of sacralized taboo attempting to exercise its influence on even the innermost feelings and desires. He is even led into distorting into a menacing taboo prohibition the words of Christ concerning the internal sins in which the Christian discovers the deepest appeal to the totality of his loving self-donation. And his primary assumption so wholly blinds him to the nature of the saint's awareness of sin, the result of a consuming love of God, that he is forced to interpret it as an extreme neurotic repression of all sound instinctivity. That is why Hesnard's interpretation will sound as mistaken to the Christian who authentically experiences his inner shaping by grace as the reproach that he lets himself be tyrannized by the whims of his wife sounds to a man really in love.

As the natural law must express itself within the concrete community of men in moral rules and principles, so too the inner law of the Holy Spirit must assume a *tangible shape* within the community of the Church. For God's invitation not only takes hold of man at the highest point of his spirit but encompasses him in the full dimensions of his humanity; it is addressed to him both in the sensory aspect of his being as a spirit in matter and in the relational aspect of his being as a man among men. The dialog of love between God and man will not only be carried on through an inner attraction; God's salvific utterance will be heard within the human community in signs perceptible by the senses; the prophetic words of men he has inspired, his saving intervention through the events in a chosen people's history—all this reaching a

climax in the full utterance of his incarnate Word, who came
down into our human history and lives on perpetually within
the new people of God, his everlasting Church. That Church
is the bearer of the fullness of revelation, bringing it down
through history to an ever more conscious and rich unfolding,
thus gradually preparing humanity for the final achievement
of history in Christ's return, when he will give everything
into the hands of his Father, so that God may be all in all.

The whole history of salvation is structured *sacramentally*.
What manifests itself so clearly in Christ's incarnation and
redemption will become the law of God's saving self-commu-
nication in its totality: the outer aspect will always be both
the *revealing sign* and the *mediating instrument* of the invisi-
ble working of grace. Within the Church as the great original
sacrament God will speak to us in a plurality of sacramental
signs, in the preaching of his word, in the inspiration of Holy
Scripture, in the infallible utterances of the Church's magisterium.

The ethical demands which God's invitation presents for
our human response will share this *sacramental structure*.
These demands first found expression in the law of the Old
Covenant, were uttered more fully in the message of the
prophets; thus began the gradual development which would
lead to the Beatitudes, to Christ's fulfilling of the law and his
formulation of his new commandment. Whereas the natural
law is formulated by human society, laid down and applied
in prescriptions under man's own responsibility, in the *verbalization* and the shaping of the inner law of grace the initiative
is with God, who guarantees the divine validity and authenticity of his demands through the inspiration of his prophets
and sacred writers and the human-divine sacramentality of
his own Word.

This also applies to some extent to the *further explicitation* of the Christian demands of grace within the *Church,* since she listens to learn the demands of God's love with the continual assistance and at the continual urging of the Spirit. In every believer the inner law of the Spirit is at work like a kind of connaturality with the God who speaks to him through Christ, like a kind of *power of discrimination,* a spiritual sense of touch, capable of discerning what is and what is not an authentic verbalization of God's invitation. But in the individual that power of discrimination remains fallible. Only in the sense of faith of the Church as a hierarchic community does the connaturality with the God who speaks issue in infallible certitude. The pronouncements of the Church's magisterium are the authentic testimony of this sense of faith. It is only by heeding the sense of faith of the Church that the magisterium discovers the basis for its pronouncements, and it is only in this authoritative pronouncement that the Church's sense of faith comes to the full awareness of its certitude. At certain *privileged moments* and within strictly defined limits the Church's pronouncements concerning Christian moral activity become *infallibly assured* of their divine authenticity. Within these limits the decisions of the Church participate in the absolute character of God's own speaking and possess a certitude no human formulation of the natural law can ever claim for itself. Against such pronouncements, every assault of autonomous reason, every appeal to a personal charismatic intuition of the demands of grace, becomes senseless within the Christian perspective.

If, in this connection, there can be a "development" of morality, this can take place only in the same sense and within the same limits as hold for the development of dogma. As for dogma itself, every modification through additions or enrichment from without is excluded. The development can only consist in the *explicitation* of a fullness which was present from the beginning and which gradually reveals its implications and virtualities more fully with the evolving existence of mankind. Development also occurs in the sense of a gradually clearer *distinction* between the core of the evangelical and ecclesial messages and the *presentation* or formulation of them, which may be influenced by time and circumstances.

The assistance of the Spirit in his Church does not end with the infallibly guaranteed utterances of the magisterium. It is constantly at work throughout all time in the moral thinking and feeling of Christendom as a whole, as it takes shape in what is called the Church's *tradition*. Hence, as for the content of the faith, so also with regard to moral issues, there are concentric circles of a gradually decreasing certitude which the sense of faith and the thinking of individuals will take into account. When, for instance, on points which are not explicitly mentioned in the Gospels or defined by the Church's pronouncements, the Church's sense of faith has nevertheless spoken out with perfect unanimity over the centuries, would not the rejection of such an opinion on the sole grounds of some personal feeling or some personal argument be an obvious sign that one was taking oneself too seriously? Only in a respectful listening to tradition and a reverent inquiry into the Church's sense of faith, as it lived in the past, is there hope that, when new problems arise, we may be able to sift, in the traditional conceptions, what belongs to the content of revelation from that which is of the times, and thus promote rather than hinder an authentic development of Christian ethics.

Yet a clear distinction must be made between tradition in the sense intended above and the so-called *traditional concepts* of *moral theology*. Like dogmatic theology, moral theology is in the first place a science which constructs its positions under the guidance of faith, yet on *its own responsibility*. Hence the opinions of the moralists offer no other guarantee in the domain of faith than the degree of certainty of intelligently inquiring scholars working under the guidance of their own experience of the faith and trying to keep attuned to the sense of faith of the whole Church. That is why, although their investigations offer welcome material and useful tools for the development of the moral insight of the faith, the path over which the Church's sense of faith reaches its certitudes is not necessarily marked out by their scientific conclusions, and it is not bound by them.

Besides the embodiment of the inner demands of God's grace in a Christian moral law, the Church also needs a general organization of the individual efforts and free initiatives of the children of God for the common good. Hence the Church too will have a complete system of *positive law*, always influenced by the working of God's grace but lacking any divine guarantee—essentially subject, therefore, to the relativity characterizing all human legislation and to the same limitations. The prescriptions of the Church, too, may turn out to be arbitrary, or lag behind the life of the Church, or give rise to grievous abuses. The normal need for reform in the Church, felt so strongly, for instance, on the occasion of the present Council, will usually operate more specifically on the level of positive legislation, where the Church enjoys no divine guarantee.

THE CHRISTIAN CONSCIENCE BEFORE THE LAW

The foregoing considerations with regard to the law may have shown one thing very clearly: that it does not make sense to talk in a general way (as happens too often) about the relation between "the" Christian conscience and "the" law. That relation varies very considerably, not only according to the level of law and the kind of law in question, but also according to whether the Christian conscience confronting the law is mature and adult.

1. The Adult Christian Conscience

We should perhaps begin with the attitude of the *adult* Christian conscience before the law in its several aspects. The first thing to be said is that in *principle* there can be no opposition between an adult conscience and the law, hence that an opposition in *principle* to the law cannot be a fundamental attitude of the Christian conscience. For maturity of conscience means the conscious welcoming of the direction of one's own development and God's invitation within his Church. It implies a free decision to become fully what one is through one's human abilities and the divine calling. But the law's only aim is to express and clarify the implications of that direction and that calling. Hence in principle the adult person will acknowledge and welcome in the law the imperative of his own striving towards human and Christian adulthood, even though he may be clearly aware of the imperfections in its formulation and thus of the corrections he must introduce into it. To be in principle hostile and opposed to every law may safely be considered an infallible sign of immaturity.

Ideal spiritual adulthood of the conscience would consist in this: that the compass of love would point the direction so unfalteringly that the *external law* is no longer needed. In such a man the law has been so fully assimilated, its deepest inspiration is so much a matter of personal experience, that it has become a conscious instinct and an infallible power of discrimination.[30] This power would automatically sift in the law what is an authentic expression of the person's own growth imperative and of the divine calling from what is unadapted, only human and imperfect, which is to be eliminated if he is to remain or become fully himself in loving self-donation.

Something like this adulthood may undoubtedly be seen, if not at the start, at least in the autumn of some saintly lives. In them the "Love and do as you will" of Augustine finds the fullness of its meaning.

But such a maturity of love is rather rare and cannot be considered the usual situation of the average Christian conscience. To say nothing of all the opportunities of growth we have neglected in our own past through weakness and cowardice, the education of most of us as human beings and as Christians has been far from perfect, and a vast number of potentialities have never been developed in us. Authentic adulthood involves also the humble *acknowledgment* of what has *remained infantile* in ourselves, of our bondage to our own past, of all the subjective projections which color and distort our picture of objective reality. Moreover, the adult Christian knows that deeper even than these personal failures and immaturities is *concupiscence*, the lasting repercussion in him, even after the grace of baptism, of the situation of original sin in which he is caught as a child of man and from which he must allow himself to be ever more perfectly saved. He is all too often made painfully aware of how far short his own spiritual stature falls of the full adult stature of Christ and

how awfully little the human race, whose life he shares, thinks
and reacts in a Christian way.

When he faces a decision of conscience, the adult Christian
will not evade his responsibility by depending blindly on the
letter of the law. But he will *listen* with gratitude to what the
law can provide as a correction of his own views and as a
safeguard against the deforming influence of his drives and
prejudices. And more than any law he will take the *Person
of Christ* as his norm, adopt him as a model and as the test
of authenticity.

In the inner law of nature, in the inner demands of God's
spirit, in the pronouncements and gestures of the Church, as
guaranteed by God, he will unconditionally rediscover the
imperative of his own conscience, for he knows that true love
cannot contradict itself. Yet as the applications of the law of
nature or of grace which he meets in his life become further
removed from the very first principles, the influences of the
concrete *factors which make up his situation* and of the insight
of the person living in that situation keep increasing. This
is especially true when it must be decided whether some
positive law obliges in a specific instance.

Within these limits—and although the term has acquired a
bad reputation because of the abuses to which it has led—
we must clearly affirm with the great classical authors that
Catholic morality is, in fact, a *situation ethics*. Once a man
has sufficiently formed his conscience by attending to the law
of nature and of grace, by purifying his intention and gather-
ing solid information, there comes a moment when God's
personal invitation in the concrete situation is something no
mere legality can wholly discern.

The final act in which the will to action faces the object in
its irreducible concreteness, with all its aspects of pondering,

deliberating, and finally deciding, belongs to the essentially practical virtue of prudence.[31]

Textbook morality of the last centuries was obviously so wary of the dangers involved in the personal, prudential character of the ultimate decision of conscience, that it endeavored to foresee all possible situations and to spell out in advance the application of the law for each one of these "cases." Such *casuistry* necessarily remains in the realm of theory and abstraction, never getting beyond objective, anonymous and impersonal data. But in the situation I am myself at stake, in a unique pattern of subjective conditions and objective data which cannot be foreseen or described.* Every priest has had this brought home to him by his own bewilderment when hearing his first confessions; for years he has studied "cases," now he faces "situations." Even the best pastoral theology cannot bridge that gap. Ultimately the decision comes from the personal conscience. That conscience must be followed and respected, even when, after honestly inquiring and examining the law—in good faith—it errs in its judgment.

2. The Immature Christian Conscience

The relation between a conscience which is *still immature* and the law is quite another matter. For real liberty stands at

---

* In S. Andres' novel *Wir sind Utopia* (1943) the fallen-away monk Paco, having been caught by the Communists and locked up in the monastery where he used to live, meets a Russian lieutenant who has observed that he is a priest and asks him to hear his confession. Paco has managed to keep a knife, and when he hears that all the prisoners are about to be executed he wonders whether, after the confession, it would be allowable for him to kill the lieutenant. The anguish which grips him before this decision makes him feel existentially the difference between a concrete situation and the "cases" he used to study and decide with so much assurance.

the end of education, not at the beginning. The more immature the conscience is the more it needs the prop of a law
from outside, because the inner orientation is not yet capable
of finding its path through the unintegrated turmoil of the
passions. The sapling needs a prop to keep it from growing
crooked. For the essence of immaturity consists in the lack of
personal integration.

Everyone will admit this so far as the young child is concerned. But even for the further development of the individual
and the group the support of the external law remains to a
large extent indispensable. That *pedagogical* character of the
law is illustrated by the whole history of Israel; it is an important theme in St. Paul's discussion of the opposition between
Jewish law and Christian liberty.[32]

Perhaps the most delicate task in education is making sure
that the growing dialog of dependence and autonomy will
take place as harmoniously as possible, so that personality
may always receive full scope without the danger of a premature removal of the sheltering dependence on the law leading
to bewilderment and helplessness.

However, even the best education must keep in mind that
human development, like every process of growth, is not
continuous, but occurs by leaps and bounds. Hence *critical
moments* cannot be avoided, and the kind of prudence that
would prevent them at any cost would lead to a pernicious
infantilism. Almost unavoidably a time comes when the
capacity for autonomy falls short of the impassioned will for
autonomy. At such a time the craving for adulthood cannot
but manifest itself in the form of rebellion against the law.
One wants to get rid of its exacting assistance even though
one cannot yet safely rely on one's own wisdom and responsibility. The fledgling cannot wait until its wings are strong
before giving up the safety of the nest.

What is called a free decision of conscience in such circumstances will often be an ambiguous mixture of good intentions and all kinds of uncontrolled urges and desires. The
vague feeling of anxiety aroused by that ambiguity is shaken
off with an appeal to *subjective sincerity*, which remains the
final moral norm. But the word sincerity is capable of ambiguity too. There is a *spiritual* sincerity, a quiet fidelity to the
known truth. And there is an *emotional* sincerity, deriving
from the mood of the moment and more or less consciously
allowing all kinds of feelings and impulses to help shape one's
vision of reality. One can then—as in so many declarations of
love, outbursts of anger and political statements, so in one's
decisions of conscience—"sincerely mean it," or "tell it sincerely in the way one means it." Yet later on, in another mood
or in other affective circumstances, one can claim with equal
"sincerity": "Of course, I did not mean it that way." The "ethic
of the heart" to which the immature individual likes to appeal
in opposition to the cold, objective morality of the law is often
based more on emotional than on spiritual sincerity. Hence it
easily degenerates into fickleness, shallowness and arbitrariness. Here too education should not condemn that ambiguous
attitude outright; it must take hold of the authentic will for
spiritual sincerity and detach it from the unauthentic, often
blind, emotionality in whose grip it still is.[33]

Physical and moral adulthood do not necessarily go together.
A person may be an adult physically, he may even have
delicate perceptions, a broad intellectual culture and a capacity for acute psychological introspection, yet remain *morally
a child*—that is, in his commitment to life. We have explained
in an earlier chapter why the circumstances of modern life
make it difficult to become an adult in that sense. Hence it
may be expected that there are a considerable number of
people, adults in the physical and cultural sense, who have

never had the courage to make the leap into moral autonomy, either because their education never gave them the opportunity or because, when the chance was given, their anxiety was in the end greater than their courage.

The crisis of growth into adulthood may never occur in such people, because life lets them go about their business in their infantile moral world without too much trouble. In a world which is developing with such great impetus as ours, cases like these will become more exceptional: a humanity become more adult demands more from each adult individual. And it is almost inevitable that the conflict between one's task and one's commitment will ultimately reach a state of crisis. Frequently circumstances will bring about a crisis at a *later age.* It will then have a more painful and frightening course of development, since the psychic complexity to be integrated is much greater and responsibilities are much heavier than at the usual age of puberty.

This can have far-reaching effects. For some most important life decisions are bound to specific legal requirements, and for these legal norms, whether of the Church or of civil society, it is not possible to judge of adulthood by any but externally perceptible criteria. Thus the marriage laws of the Church take for granted that the sincerely meant Yes pronounced at his wedding in adult age by a person considered normal expresses an adult decision of conscience. The fact of the matter, however, is that many marriage conflicts—many more than one might think—have their origin in the morally immature, infantile way in which people who are legally adults approach that sacrament.

Moral and religious adulthood likewise are not necessarily parallel. A person who is well-developed morally may be deficient in love, whereas a profound, authentic love of God may develop into adult holiness despite moral infantilisms it never quite succeeds in overcoming. In St. Paul's Epistles the distinction between maturity as a human being and as a Christian is a frequently recurring theme. In this connection one may wonder whether, in many of our contemporaries, the sympathy for situation ethics is not the expression of a very profound resistance to the unconditional character of the total donation to God's love, which forces one out of every natural shelter; whether it does not mean an anxious effort to keep one's vital decisions within one's own autonomous power. In that case it would only be an expression of the scandal of all times before the paradox of Christian adulthood: that he who wishes to save his life shall lose it, but he who is willing to lose it saves it forever.

All that has been said here of personal adulthood largely applies also to the gradual *reaching of adulthood of mankind*. Mankind too must regularly pass through times of crisis. And we may wonder whether the present situation, as described at the beginning of this chapter, has not a remarkable resemblance to the crisis of adolescence.*

It is as if man, after living in too close quarters, unable to conceive of his humanity except in terms of certain definite forms of civilization and cultural patterns, had suddenly, in a world becoming one on a planetary scale, been confronted with the question of what "man" might really be. Full of the

---

*On modern man in search of his image, see the pertinent remarks of J. M. Domenach, "L'homme de demain," in *L'annonce de l'évangile aujourd'hui* (Paris, 1963), pp. 192–221. On the "youth" of the Church, "an adolescent who has not yet reached the full development of adulthood," an excellent discussion in H. Fesquet's *Catholicisme, religion de demain?* (Paris, 1962), pp. 219–223.

passionate preoccupation with self and the all-encompassing curiosity of adolescence, he sees a chance of divesting himself of all that particularizes him, all that binds him to space and time, in order to discover, in himself and in others, the image of man in its original authenticity. It is noteworthy that the hero of modern drama, of the film and the novel, is no longer the extraordinary person or one who lives in extraordinary circumstances, but the most ordinary man, one who has nothing special to recommend him but the fact that he is a human being—the average consumer of the economist, the anonymous statistic, the man of the serial, of hit-parade love and of nameless, simple loneliness. No longer even "modern" man or "man as such," but, coming from East or from West, from megalopolis or hamlet, from the president's chair or out of the breadline, simply "man." And the questions and problems which literature, film and stage treat are not accidental conflicts but, under the most diverse forms, always the basic question about the meaning of his existence and the authentic status of his being man. The genesis of this self-awareness shows all the signs which mark the self-discovery of puberty: a strong subjectivity, restless self-analysis, rejection of all traditions and bonds, a combination of anxiety and cocksure self-assertion, attempts at retreat towards the shelter of childhood and a reckless advance towards new points of view.

The Church too is beginning to realize that her Christianity is still in its childhood. The Church too is passing through a crisis of growth which is influenced and intersected by that of mankind. She too must emerge from Mediterranean civilization, that narrow environment of her earlier years. She must cease to avoid the risks of evolving worldwide events, abandon the paternalistic forms of colonizing missionary activity, in order to become fully a world-Church, a home for "man" in all his cultures and forms of life. In her case also this stage of growth is attended by the undeniable signs of the boisterousness and the uneasiness of adolescence.

Might not situation ethics in the final analysis be a reflection, in the ethical consciousness of believers, of the crisis of growth through which mankind's collective consciousness is now passing? Then with all its exaggerations, it might represent an attempt, both human and Christian, to break out of the shelter of all exterior safeguards and to coincide, in a renewed and more complete self-possession, with the deepest root of one's own being and vocation. Then all those exaggerations would only be the unavoidable ransom youth pays in breaking through to adulthood, not a phenomenon of decadence but a sign of spring.

APPLICATION IN THE PASTORAL DOMAIN

In practice the problems of the relation between law, morality and grace confront the priest with a twofold task: he must try to lead Christian man and the Christian community from an infantile to an adult Christian ethics, and he must take a stand on the conflicts between the law and the individual and collective conscience of the faithful.

EDUCATION TO AN ADULT CHRISTIAN ETHICS

The question of what the priest can and should do to educate towards a more adult Christian conscience presupposes a diagnosis of the present situation of the Christian conscience and of the factors determining it.

1. The Situation

One who sets out to ascertain the average ethical level of
the ordinary Christian of our time will find little cause for
satisfaction. We must honestly admit that the Catholic conscience shows a *frightful amount of infantilism*. Every priest
in the ministry continually meets remnants of a half-magical
attitude towards guilt and sin, expressions of a legalistic taboo
mentality, which have hardly anything to do with a grasp of
the Christian calling and the need for salvation. There is
more: he constantly notices that this state of mind continues
to be promoted, consciously or unconsciously, and presented
as the real Christian ethic, by quite a number of parents or
educators who consider themselves pious Christians, and even
by priests in the ministry. If Hesnard's reproaches do not
apply to real Catholic morality, they describe very correctly
what is too often presented or practiced as such.

That infantilism is perhaps most often and most clearly
manifested on the occasion of *confession*. Among people who
are spiritually underdeveloped the point is sometimes reached
at which absolution is literally taken as a magic formula which
one tries to secure by any means available. And when the
penitent, by dint of wrapping serious sins in vague, innocent
formulas, or quickly whispering hard-to-mention sins between
two pious avowals of imperfection, has been able to deceive
the confessor, he feels quite cheerful, because once more he
has got the better of God. Even among devout souls infantilism often assumes alarming proportions. How often in
weekly or fortnightly confessions, one hears again and again
the echoes of a "guide for the confession of children" through
the mouths of adults. Or take the pious young woman who

speaks of her "little sins," or the nun who regularly adds to her confession "the sins which I might have forgotten," as some kind of magic safeguard against the accounting of an all-seeing God.

How often Christian life is treated as a congeries of practices and taboo prescriptions. The mysteries of sex life in particular, and married love, are reduced to a magic system of 'things" which are allowed or not allowed, to a sacralization of biological functions, or to morbid, obsessive attempts at some kind of psychic self-castration under the heading of "fighting against bad thoughts."

Sins are magnified, the uncertain is confessed as certain in order to escape the anxiety of a wrong self-judgment. Or, in the other direction, an acrobatic casuistry is practiced on an imaginary boundary line between mortal sin and venial sin. By distinctions of tortured subtlety the penitent succeeds in staying within the zone of venial sin—i.e., of "what one can afford."

How often the emphasis is placed, sometimes by preference, on things which are not even sinful, which only materially transgress some commandment: "I missed Mass on Sunday, but for a valid reason"; "I ate meat, I didn't fast, because circumstances made it impossible," etc.—and semi-superstitious or routine practices of a personal sort are put before the great commandments of love of God, love of others, and the duties of one's state of life. How frequently one gets the impression, from the disorderly enumeration of faults and shortcomings—often accompanied by silly computations—that there is no hierarchy of values; that the penitent who comes to put down his burden is not impelled by any desire to come home to God's love, but only by a need to "get rid" of his sins and return to a "state of grace" that is not much more than the absence of grave sins. Is frequent confession, for many people, more than a routine, a regularly recurring, hygienic reflex?

And asking for advice! How often, instead of an attempt to gain insight for his own decision, it is a turning over of the penitent's responsibility to the confessor—"He gives me 'permission' to do it in this way"—"I am 'allowed' by my confessor." Even an effort on the priest's part to induce some insight is often interrupted impatiently with: "Is it allowed or isn't it?" And with the infantile penitent there is the temptation, on the priest's side, to paternalism: insisting on dealing with all kinds of peripheral problems and not penetrating to what is religiously essential: the emphasis, often almost exclusively, on sexual sins; the unction of an impersonal homily in response to an equally impersonal confession of sins; the "Do it this way" advice and the matter-of-course acceptance and perpetuation of infantilism and permanent dependence on the part of the penitent.[34]

What comes out in this way in confession is only one manifestation of a mentality dominating the whole life of a considerable number of Christians. It is striking, for instance, how scarcely Christian *the image of God* is, not only among nominal Christians but even among what are called devout Christians. How often that image oscillates between that of a kindly Santa Claus god and that of a vengeful and punishing restorer of an inexorable "eternal order." It is almost incredible how many Christians carry deep down in their unconscious minds the anxious fear that God does not really approve of human happiness, that sooner or later every excess of happiness must be paid for or compensated for by unhappiness and sorrow. Incredible, too, how many purely natural events are felt to be a providential punishment for real or presumed sins and how, on the other hand, providence is reduced to a magic intervention in case of need. For how many Christians do religious practices turn into a kind of defense against God, a performance under contract, in terms of which he, on his side, binds himself to fend off temporal and eternal dangers? This is not to participate in a dialog of love, but to cover and insure oneself against a real meeting with the living God.

In relations with the *neighbor*, too, that state of mind comes to the fore, leading people to close themselves off in a selfish petty-bourgeois individualism, a childishly unconscious egoism which is not interested in the great social problems, which is also proof against the social sense of guilt that the best of the unbelievers experience so acutely. The ordinary Christian morality must bear much responsibility for the great scandal of the nineteenth century and for the loss by the Church of almost the entire laboring class. All too often it really was the opium of the people.* Likewise even now the needs of the underdeveloped nations awaken scarcely any reverberations among the great mass of Catholics, or any real readiness for commitment. That priests and religious often seem to be blind to the most elementary demands of social justice and lacking in any sense of social solidarity is another well-known fact that derives from the same state of mind.

It is not only in the domain of love of neighbor that the scale of values of the Christian virtues has gradually gone

---

* This is true of Continental Europe, of course, more than of the United States. Likewise, many of the strictures which follow apply more to European than to American Catholicism. On the other hand, until quite recently, European visitors in this country were amazed how little the average American Catholic seemed to care for the plight of so many of his colored fellow Americans. (Translator's note.)

more and more awry. The same is true for *many other virtues*.
It looks as if, during the past century, more and more emphasis
has been put on the childlike virtues, while the specific virtues
of the adult were often distrusted or reproduced in infantile
caricature. Overemphasis on authority under all its forms,
especially on the authority of parents and of priests; an unwarranted appeal to prudence in order to eliminate, as far as
possible, every risk, to keep young people in an artificial nest
as long as was feasible and even to keep adults within the
secure anonymity of the herd; the caricature of humility into
pusillanimity, obedience into slavishness, chastity into false
angelism, love of neighbor into a fussy concern never to hurt
anybody, selflessness into masochism. On the other hand, the
sense of honor, resoluteness, the sense of social responsibility,
honesty and sincerity, autonomy in judgment and action, self-
reliance and the wholesome readiness for taking risks: all this
was neglected. The Canadian who wanted to make Notre-
Dame-de-la-Trouille (Our Lady of Milquetoast) into the
national patron saint of his fellow Catholics has perhaps
unknowingly discovered a Catholic world devotion.[35] At the
first unexpected difficulty, the darling member of the flock
runs for advice to his confessor, who hurries to do the same
and consults a periodical or a professor.

Even the opposition to the pressure of the law very often
derives from a still wholly *legalistic state of mind*. It is an
infantile craving for independence, trying to find somewhere
some kind of permission in order to end up by doing as it
pleases. In the situation ethics of many Christians the realization hardly dawns that they become free for a deeper commitment, not for comfort or self-indulgence; free to surrender
their life more completely, not to preserve it better for themselves. The fact that the registered nurse, who is subject to

the law, can lay aside her concern for her patients once her eight hours are up, while the mother, precisely because she is free of the law, must care for her sick child day and night as long as he needs her, seems to be a form of situation ethics which has little appeal.

Many even seem to hold implicitly, as a first principle, that God has no right to expect anything out of the ordinary from the ordinary person. How many would wholeheartedly agree with the words of Karl Rahner, when he declares that a real Christian situation ethics is unthinkable without admitting "that the world stands under the *sign of the cross* to which God himself has been nailed? That it follows logically that God's commandment may demand even the death of a person; that there is no bitterness, no tragedy, no despair in the world which would be too high a price for God's eternal promise; that one may do no evil in order to reach the good; that it is an error and a heresy of a 'welfare ethics' to think that the moral good cannot put man in a tragedy which offers no outcome within the limits of this world; that, on the contrary, the Christian must expect, as almost a matter of course, that his Christian existence will bring him sooner or later into a situation in which he must give up everything so as not to lose his soul and that it is not up to man always to keep out of a 'heroic' situation. . . ."[36]

If we reject all this, does not the freedom of the children of God degenerate into the freedom of God's infants?

2. The Causes

The causes of this situation are many and complex. First there is the fact that mankind as a whole grows only very *gradually* to moral *adulthood* and that the Christian moral sense has by no means yet, even in our time, reached that of

the full stature of Christ. It is in continual conflict with the
resistance of strongly persisting primitive instincts, anxieties
and superstitions. Even where man very sincerely yields to
grace, it takes many centuries before it has taken root in
him, penetrating all his atavisms and automatisms, to the
extent that his reflexes become a reliable infrastructure for a
Christian moral and religious consciousness. A comparison, in
this respect, between Old World Christians—even fallen-away
Christians—and those of the recently founded Christian communities in Asia and Africa is very instructive.

Pharisaism too is a recurrent temptation in the religious life
of the Church, not so much in the sense of conscious hypoc-
risy as in the original meaning of a desire to rely on one's
own strength in one's relation to God. In the face of God's
inscrutability man tries to provide for himself by an accumulation of practices and performances, to force God to acknowledge his merit and give him the reward of everlasting life.
Quite naturally, then, the material aspect of the law and the
performances to be offered take precedence over one's self-
donation to God; not God but the Ego occupies the center
of the stage. And thus pharisaism leads naturally to pride,
self-importance and scorn for others who are incapable of the
same performances. That kind of pharisaism is no monopoly
of the Jewish religion. In the first centuries of the Church it
shows up again in the form of Pelagianism, and it survives
until now under all kinds of disguises. It becomes even more
deceptive in its exacting zeal, since, under the influence of
the gospel, it has appropriated the idiom of the publican.
Beating its breast and confessing its sinfulness has become
one of its favorite attitudes. The gradual secularization of
thought under external structures which remained Christian,
especially during the nineteenth century, gave a new impetus

to the deviation of religion towards that kind of quantified legalism.

A third cause undoubtedly lies in what is nowadays generally called the *anti-Reformation complex.*

The reaction against the Protestant principle of free inquiry unavoidably led, within the counter-Reformation, to an over-emphasis on dogmatic compliance and on submission to every utterance of the Church. The means used in defense of the true faith, especially the activity of the courts of the Inquisition and their institutionalization in permanent bodies like the Holy Office, could not but shut the Church in on itself in a defensive attitude in which self-preservation and a rigid traditionalism took precedence of all else. Because of the heavy Protestant attacks on Catholic practice with regard to sacraments, sacramentals and devotion to the saints, the Church had to emphasize these so much that almost inevitably the *"opus operatum"* degenerated, in the mind and practice of many, into some kind of magical automatism that slowly began to infect all the practices of piety. However much the Protestant doctrine of the total corruption of human nature by original sin had been combated and rejected by Catholics, it would nevertheless, especially later on through Jansenism, exert a very real influence upon the devotional practices and the thought of Catholicism. In many countries the anti-Reformation rigidity of ecclesiastical life would increase still further on account of the very great influence of the clergy, never disturbed throughout the last century by any serious persecution. That influence often prevailed almost as much in the secular as in the religious domain; in a troubled and changing world it came to consider itself more and more as the defender by natural right of the existing order, as the unchallenged sovereign of consciences and as the local omnipresence of God's own authority. The organizational ramifications through which this ecclesiastical paternalism penetrated into the most remote corners of secular life rendered its grasp almost unescapable during the last century for those who had remained Christians.

Secular culture as well (and this is a fourth important cause of the present situation) has until quite recently accepted *paternalism* as the obvious and the only possible model for the social order, as is again and again demonstrated in colonialism, education and politics. For bourgeois morality, of which the welfare state is only a perpetuation in disguise, aims mainly at security against all the possible risks of life. Whether the attempt is made to reach this individually, as in European liberalism, or collectively, in socialized institutions, the craving for security is always the dominating factor. The administrative apparatus tries, even more systematically than ecclesiastical legislation, more and more to encompass all individual cases through a proliferation of laws. It must be admitted that nowadays the Church manifests a power of adaptation and a respect for particular differences and needs which many a secular organization might well try to emulate.

3. Re-Education to Adult Morality

Re-educating the physically and culturally adult Christian to greater maturity in the taking of moral decisions is certainly an urgent task of the pastoral ministry. Yet what can be achieved in that respect is naturally very limited, because at that age the psyche no longer has the plasticity and the vitality which would make possible a general breakthrough of a new moral attitude. This will probably take place only among a spiritual elite, and the new atmosphere thus generated might be caught by the mass of the people, so that they too might begin to breathe more freely. However, the prospect of a greater maturity of conscience on the part of people in general is, for the time being, rather a hope for the distant future and presupposes, above all, a new approach in the education of the younger generations, the adults of the future.

a. The Child

Education to adult morality should begin in the *very first years of life*.[37] First in the manner in which the *authority* of the parents and of the other educators meets the emerging consciousness and the growing will for life of the child. We don't mean that the child should be left entirely on his own resources from the start, that one should "let him have his own way, for fear he should get complexes," as one hears rather naively said today. Quite the contrary: for in that case the child in his helplessness would be navigating in a sea so full of unknown perils, always unexpected and overwhelming, that he would begin to build a structure of taboos, to protect himself, which might eventually turn into a superego far more tyrannical than the sternest parental authority. Actually the child will be afforded all the opportunities he needs only within the shelter of a love that is solicitous, protective and strong, through which the risks of life are kept in proportion to his size, so that his facing of life can take place in normal stages in pace with his developing powers.

It would therefore be a fatal mistake to try, as it were, to skip the superego stage in the formation of the young conscience. The superego is necessary; the child cannot do without it. However, it depends to a great extent on the parents whether, in relation to the later development of conscience, that superego will be a permanent prison or the protecting shell which opens at the right moment.

The *superego* can be a *preparation for life* only if the drilling by authority—the habits, reflexes and thought schemas cultivated—is so much a prefiguration of what the child, aware of the thrust of growth, experiences as his own vital law, that he will not have to scrap his childish morality, but only to personalize it in order to achieve a harmonious personality. For this purpose the parents, in exercising their authority, must not take themselves as a norm, but only the personal development of their children. In other words, they must never command anything because *they* need it, but only because their *child* needs it. How often the rest and comfort of the "grown ups" is forced as a norm upon the wholesome spontaneity of the child! How frequently orders are given inspired only by the nervousness or the anxiety or the pride or the mutual jealousy of father and mother! How often the personal disappointments, unfulfilled wishes, frustrations, anxieties and aggressivity are projected on the child in what are called decisions about his education! This is the vicious circle in the process of education to maturity: immature parents cannot educate children to maturity. Only a mature authority can enter into a dialog with the immature and, without giving way, leave full scope for, and stimulate, that which is growing towards real maturity in the young being. Even in the case of the small child, the famous "Why? Because. That's why!" is rarely the last word of authority; generally it is the last recourse of a failing education.

It might therefore be good to skip the usual hymn to *maternal love* for a few years. Not because it is not a marvelous reality, but because the word has acquired too ambiguous a meaning. For it may mean the maternal instinct as well as fully developed mother love. True, the maternal instinct is wholly devoted to the care of the child, but driven by its own need for satisfaction, which it finds in this caring. Hence it views the child as a precious possession to be defended with tooth and claw against robbery, even if the thief is life itself or love. Real mother love, on the other hand, is a gradual letting go of the child on behalf of life. And Christian motherhood is an experience of that letting go as the most perfect feminine expression of one's own surrender to the love and the life of God. Although the hymn to motherhood is, we presume, intended for Christian motherhood, it is in fact misappropriated by too many mothers to give full rein, under a safe Christian label, to an instinctive, often monstrously possessive, motherliness.

Quite a number of other pedagogical terms—obedience, gratitude, self-control, generosity, etc.—would gain much from a demythologizing that would rid them of the dangerous ambiguity in which the usual jargon of piety keeps them imprisoned.

What has been said of moral education is true *a fortiori* of *religious-Christian education*. Only to the extent that the love, the authority, the harmonious relations between the parents mirror God's love for their children, intimate, sheltering, strong and all-demanding; only to the extent that they refrain from monopolizing their children's love but refer it beyond themselves to a supreme love sheltering them all together and bearing them up—only to that extent can their educational influence, perpetuated in the child's soul by the superego, be an anticipating prefiguration in the child's psyche of the adult religious self-donation.

Along with the affective context of pre-personal moral experience, which remains the most important factor, *explicit moral education*—the formation of habits, reward and punishment, the development of insight, moral and religious instruction, the practice of confession and so on—is often also of decisive importance. It is generally admitted that in this respect also there is much need for improvement. Here again, however, the effort to find a more authentic way of speaking of heaven and hell, sin and penance, a modified practice of confession, should not make us wish to skip the superego stage or to wait with real formation of conscience until that stage has come to an end. Anyone who, under the pretext of a later free choice for the children, would deny the parents all right to a previous option, would at once render all education impossible. He might as well have the children select their own diet! The more deeply the values involved in the choice affect the very core of existence, the more unavoidable a pre-option on the part of the parents becomes, because education is entirely based on these values. Although the moral experience of the child remains largely implicit within instinctive taboo reactions, and although, as a consequence, religious instruction can be experienced only under a mythologized form and the practice of the sacraments only within a still semi-magical state of mind, this is not a sufficient reason to refrain from speaking of sin, heaven and hell before the age of puberty or for putting off the first confession until that time. Both must be adapted to the mental state of these years, so that the developing consciousness may rest on a solid foundation. It is very true that quite a number of people no longer go to confession later in life because in their childhood they experienced confession as a form of coercion, or as something frightening. This demonstrates that they learned in the wrong way to go to confession or that they had to approach the sacrament with an affective attitude which had already been thoroughly distorted. But how many people would be unable really to go to confession if they started to go only at an adult age, without any connection with the affective experiences of childhood? Was the religion of primitive humanity less authentic because it was still in the grip of an infantile-magical attitude? And what would our personal religion be like without the whole instinctive substratum inherited from our forebears?

b. The Adolescent

A very important, indeed a critical, moment in the education towards religious maturity occurs in the *years of adolescence.*[38] Important because the basic attitudes into which the emerging personality settles during these years will constitute the basis of his adult conception of life. Critical because, between the onset of adulthood in the physical and psychological domain and the spiritual unfolding of the personality, occurs a *psychological vacuum* of quite some duration, in which the growing youth is no longer enough of a child to accept the attitude of authority, and not yet enough of an adult to arrange his life wholly on his own responsibility. The fact that nowadays physiological puberty occurs about one full year earlier than it did two generations ago, whereas spiritual and characterological adulthood occurs not earlier but somewhat later than formerly, renders the problem posited by that vacuum even more acute. Unsolved problems and conflict situations of the first years of life, which scarcely manifested themselves in any perceptible way during the so-called latency period of childhood, now surge ahead with renewed violence; they increase the confusion of the adolescent and make him more difficult for his educators to understand.

However much the adolescent may seem to wish to shake off every influence of his educators, the fact is that he is never

so liable to be *really influenced* as during these years, and
that influence will be decisive for the positions he will adopt
as an adult. More, however, than advice or instruction, the
personality of the educator will influence him. For he is
looking for somebody towards whom he may lift himself up
in admiration, a model for the molding of his growing personality, a rock of certitude in the whirlpool of his moods,
doubts and questions. If the educator is, so to speak, on the
same wavelength as the young man, he can enter into a dialog
with him, challenge him to become an adult at those moments
when, in discouragement, he feels like letting himself slip back
into childhood; let him see, as in a mirror, the authenticity or
unauthenticity of his efforts to become a man (or a woman),
encourage him and stimulate him, by just being there, in every
authentic self-affirmation.

If the educator wants to succeed in his task, he should be
especially careful not to take some things too literally, but to
search for their meaning within the context of the global
psychology of youth. How can he help the young person to
become himself if he sees unbridled arrogance in a rebelliousness which is often only a desperate resistance to a helpless
sense of constriction; if, behind the most emphatic black-or-
white assertions, he is not aware of the request for clarification, not presented as a request, lest the youth's uncertainty
be shown up; if, in the criticisms levelled against our Mother
the Church, he does not see the boy's clumsy effort to free
himself in a symbolic way of his own mother image; if, in
youthful idealism, he cannot distinguish between a real urge
for self-donation and a flight from reality? Treating symptoms
is generally fatal at that age; only *understanding in depth* can
really help. This is perhaps most true for sexual problems,
which seem to dominate everything in the young man's field

of attention and which often occupy the attention of educators too exclusively. One often gathers from young people and their educators the impression that at that age everything depends on sexuality, whereas, on the contrary, sexuality at that age more than ever, depends on all the rest. For like all other phenomena, or more perhaps than all others, the sexual conduct of the young man is a symbol and a symptom. One can learn all about his deepest affective problems from the manner in which he discovers sexuality and integrates it, or fails to integrate it, in his growing personality. And generally it is only by putting order into his affectivity that he will be able to become a real adult in the sexual domain.

Hence everything is deforming at that age which has the aim of maintaining the growing consciousness on a *childish level* or *pushes it back* towards childish forms of experience: nagging investigation of the youth's intimate life; compulsion in the reception of the sacraments; moral sermonizing; submerging the individual in mere herd discipline; anxiety-generating overemphasis on the dangers of life, especially the dangers of sex and human love; the quantitative multiplication of prayers, instructions in morals, and what are thought of as character-forming readings; the artificial kindling of youthful idealism in a way that is quite out of touch with the possibilities offered by reality, and so on. But equally deforming is all that which, under the pretext of encouraging autonomy, is in fact an *encouragement of narcissistic needs* at the expense of more oblative values: playing with the young people in an infantilizing way (generally the result of some kind of nostalgia for youth on the part of the educator, who thus fulfills the unfulfilled aspirations of his own youth); that naive "understanding" (received by the young people themselves with a pitying smile) of those adults who shout

approval of all these youths ever think of; the harmful encouragement given to the shallow aspirations of youth at the expense of the deeper needs. All that really educates, on the
contrary, which goes down to the *sources* of the young person's being and takes hold of the deepest cravings for maturity,
assisting its development by helping the dream to ripen into
action; good will into resolution; spontaneity into creativity;
recklessness into courage; the yearning for tenderness into the
commitment of love; self-affirmation into self-donation; sincerity of feeling into honesty of life—and whatever invites the
young person to pay for this growth the full, undiminished
price.

c. The Adult

What can be done for the re-education of adults in the
sphere of moral decision? The discussion of problems of conscience and the clarification of ideas about law and conscience
which take place in sermons, discussion groups, centers for
religious formation, and so on, can undoubtedly contribute
greatly to the maturation of consciences. Yet no automatic
results may be expected from *intellectual instruction*. It would
be a great pity if the universal mania for instruction should
also spread to the field of formation of conscience. The difficulties which inhibit an adult decision of conscience are in
part, but not exclusively or even predominantly, of an intellectual nature, and a theoretical realization of the irrationality
of anxieties, doubts and inhibitions is not enough to remove
them. One does not render a man autonomous by telling him
that he ought to be, however forcefully and emphatically one
may tell him so and whatever the strength of the arguments
employed.

There is even a danger that throwing a man too abruptly back onto his own solitary personal resources in the matter of responsibility should increase his anxiety and helplessness rather than remove them. The complaints of the best lay people in this respect sometimes have a rather bitter sound. The same people, they argue, who have kept us from making decisions, and under tutelage, throughout our whole past life now tell us that we have been wrong. Instead of acknowledging their own mistakes as educators, and joining with us in a search for a more mature attitude, they demand that we shall show an immediate and total maturity in matters of conscience. And they do so with the same cocksureness, the same authoritarian, schoolmasterly abstractness, with the same lack of real companionship, with which they formerly taught us just the opposite. The very ones who frightened us away from the water now dare us to dive at once, at the first attempt, from the highest board; but they themselves remain safely on shore.

The reproach is not always unfounded. At any rate, it is an invitation for the priest to examine his own maturity, to proceed gradually in his educational efforts, and especially to be humbly co-operative with the faithful.

In the personal *non-directive conversation,* treated in the foregoing chapter, the priest has an opportunity to fulfill all these conditions. His listening attention must be experienced by his visitor as total co-operation with him and as unconditioned faith in his capacities for growing to maturity; otherwise non-directive listening turns into the worst form of authoritarianism. The priest applies no pressure, does nothing in the place of the partner, but is for him, by the very quality of his presence, a continual invitation to express himself wholly and, in this total expression, to grow towards himself. Here, then, we have the best-adapted possibility for a real development towards moral maturity.

When the penitent asks for advice *on the occasion of confession*, the same possibilities are not offered; if for no other reason, at least because the time for such a conversation is not available. This is one more reason for separating pastoral counseling from the sacramental remission of sins. In practice, however, most advice is still sought on the occasion of confession, and the priest should also use that opportunity for the re-education of the adult towards moral maturity. In order to attain this, he will have to resist the temptation to take the moral decision into his own hands with an apodictical answer and hand it down to the penitent as a ready-made solution.

A factor that often plays a decisive role in the education towards maturity of the decisions of conscience is the ability to make for oneself a clear *distinction* between the *feeling of guilt* and the *awareness of guilt*. It is possible, as we explained in the first chapter, for the blind warning signal of the feeling of guilt to have been put completely out of kilter by all kinds of mistakes in our education or traumatic experiences. It may arise with great intensity in connection with actions in which there is no moral guilt whatsoever and be totally lacking when serious moral faults are in question. Hence it is important that a man should know enough about himself to be able to judge to what extent he can rely on his spontaneous feeling of guilt in determining his moral guilt and to what extent his conscience must ignore that feeling of guilt in order to arrive at a correct evaluation of his actions.

This becomes especially clear in the borderline case of

scrupulosity. What the scrupulous person is trying to do is precisely this: to rid himself on the moral level, by reasoning, of an anxiety for guilt which is situated on a wholly different level, the instinctive. Hence the total uselessness of his efforts: the weighing of the objective data is continually upset by the anxiety which falsifies the weights. Therefore reasoning with a scrupulous person leads nowhere; all motivated exhortations to be at peace glance off the irrational feeling of panic. It is only when the scrupulous person begins to discover the distinction between those two levels and realizes the senselessness of his efforts to allay an instinctive reaction with moral arguments, that he becomes able to keep his moral decision to some extent out of the grip of his anxiety by handing it over to somebody else, while he uses the relative rest thus obtained for a treatment of the anxiety complex itself.

Even when no scrupulosity is involved, people are far more often *victims* of a *feeling of guilt* in their moral judgments than they realize. Especially in women, who judge intuitively more than by reasoning, this turning of the awareness of guilt into an instinctive feeling of guilt is an ever-present threat, and the distinction between the two should be carefully explained to them. Thus, again, in sexual experiences, a domain in which the physical feeling of guilt—with all the added strength it picks up from a mere taboo education and wrong sexual instruction—is a far from reliable gauge of value, the instinctive feeling is nevertheless continually employed as a norm. The rather prudish girl who justifies sexual relations with her fiancé as a matter of course with the claim, "Why, isn't it beautiful? We love each other truly, what's wrong with it?", unintentionally starts from the hypothesis that what is sexually wrong is the same thing as what is filthy and repulsive. That an expression of love which humanly speaking may be as perfect before as after the wedding can be a sin, because marriage—from the human, and especially from the Christian, point of view is so much more than the yielding to a beautifully human attraction for each other—that is not included in instinctive feeling and remains wholly out of consideration. In many other fields similar deviations occur. Cleansing the awareness of guilt from contamination with irrational feelings of guilt appears to be an essential task of the priest in the reeducation of the Christian conscience.

A last, but a very important, condition for the maturation of consciences is out of the priest's hands, being in the province of the *hierarchical authority* in the Church. Only the Church authorities can check the rabbinical proliferation of ecclesiastical legislation, inherited from the counter-Reformation, and bring it back to decent proportions. The pressure of laws worked out into extreme details can be brought back to something which modern man can bear only through a drastic simplification. More and more the writings of moral theologians begin to emphasize, as Fr. Huizing puts it, that "the more the law itself goes down into details and casuistry, the less adapted it is to the countless variations of personal circumstances and personal religious states of mind."[39] The simplifications introduced of late in quite a number of items of ecclesiastical legislation and the trend manifesting itself in the present Council justify some optimism in this respect.

Although the demand for it is made chiefly by men, the need for escaping preventive incarceration within the framework of innumerable laws is perhaps most necessary for woman. By nature she is not made to accomplish specific, clearly defined things, but rather to allow life itself to grow and develop. In a too narrow rule of conduct set down in advance, she feels restricted in her spontaneous creativity and nearness to life, and she becomes enervated. The effects of this are felt in the masculine world as well, because it is precisely woman's influence which keeps awake in man's analytical and organizing mentality a sense of the deepest fundamental trend of his nature.

THE PRIEST CONFRONTING THE DISSENTING MORAL JUDGMENT OF THE BELIEVER

As moral judgment grows in maturity, unavoidably it will more often occur that the decision of conscience reached by the believer in certain circumstances will not conform to what the priest believes to be the right decision, or even to what the law of the Church explicitly proposes. What should the priest do in such cases? We consider here only the *priest* in his different functions; others who have to perform similar tasks will easily apply to themselves what is explained in these pages.

1. Rejection of a Specific Interpretation of the Law or of Its Applicability within a Certain Situation

It may happen that the conscience of the believer does not reject a law of the Church or an application of the natural law generally admitted within the Church, but that he gives it an *interpretation* which differs from the one the priest feels he must give it. When both interpretations are held by competent people and the Church has not taken a stand, it is evident that the priest has no right to force one of the two opinions upon the believer because of his own personal conviction. That seems obvious, but experience demonstrates that it may be useful to remind some priests of it. If the believer's interpretation is entirely new, one will have to decide on the basis of his competence in the field, his religious sincerity and the value of his arguments, the extent to which his position represents a carefully thought-out, really mature judgment of conscience, which must be respected, or a mere subjective arbitrariness, against which the general moral sense of the Church should be quietly upheld.

When the difference of opinion refers not to the interpretation of the law, but to its *applicability* within a certain situation, one must take the personal moral insight even more into account, because one is entering the domain of the "situation," which can never be entirely grasped objectively. If the priest is confronted by a mature judgment and there are no evident indications of bad faith, he cannot but unconditionally respect the personal insight. If he thinks that the point of view defended is based on a wrong evaluation of certain data, or fails to take some factors of the situation sufficiently into account, he shall try, in dialog with his penitent (or the person who is consulting him), to clarify the latter's insight. Should he cling to his opinion, the interpretation of the priest may not be forced upon him in an authoritarian fashion. His feeling for his own situation contains incommunicable elements which may ultimately determine his judgment: it is more probable that his insight is right than that the priest's is. If it should appear that the penitent or visitor is ethically immature, the priest may discreetly intimate the superiority of his own insight; never, however, at the expense of an authentic decision of conscience, if it has already been reached by the other person. In cases of doubt it will generally be wiser to decide in favor of freedom.

The most difficult situations are those in which the law and its usual interpretations are admitted, but its applicability to the person's own situation is denied, whereas that *applicability* has been officially attested by an *ecclesiastical pronouncement* or decision. An example may be clearer here than theoretical considerations.

Someone believes, for instance, that he knows with irrefutable evidence for his own conscience that his former Church wedding was invalid. But he has been unable to demonstrate this conclusively before the ecclesiastical court, or he has unexpectedly seen his suit end in a negative decision (perhaps, if we want to present an extreme case, through some guilty negligence on the part of one of the judges). He knows that the verdict of the ecclesiastical tribunal is covered by no divine or ecclesiastical guarantee of infallibility; it possesses the very human fallibility of every juridical sentence. The Church does not even declare that there certainly has been a marriage, but only that the marriage must continue to be treated as valid juridically. Yet that sentence is absolutely binding in this sense: that no new marriage may be contracted in the eyes of the Church, even though the person considers himself in conscience—rightly, perhaps—free of every previous marriage bond. Hence this man does not reject the marriage legislation of the Church. He admits, perhaps, that the severity of the juridical demands of the Church could not be relaxed without opening the door to abuses which would practically do away with the indissolubility of marriage. Precisely for that reason he feels that he is allowed in conscience to grasp the only emergency solution available to him, that of a civil wedding. For canon law that marriage will be invalid, and he will be a public sinner in the eyes of the rest of the faithful. In order to avoid the scandal involved, he might perhaps move to a part of the city where he is less well known. In his conscience, however, he knows that he is free, and he considers himself in God's eyes married in a Christian way—hence, in fact, sacramentally—in the only manner available to him.

When the priest comes into contact with this man and, after a careful and precise examination of the situation, finds out that not only is he in good faith, but also that he has persuasive reasons for considering his first marriage invalid, what should he do? Will he consider the juridical sentence of the Church as absolutely binding also on the plane of the personal meeting of conscience—in the confessional, for instance—and regard this man as living in concubinage? Or is he allowed to respect the distinction which the conscience of this believer thinks it may make between juridical and personal conscience (even though he might not approve of it) to such an extent that, in the public domain (*in foro externo,* as the moralists put it) he should fully respect the juridical decision of the Church, but in the domain of the strict personal conscience of the sacramental meeting with Christ occurring without any danger of scandal (*in foro interno*) he would allow him to act according to his conscience?

One sees at once how a rash application of the second formula might have catastrophic consequences for the common welfare, hence how, at any rate, extreme caution is required. This does not mean, however, that theoretically the second position is indefensible.

2. *Rejection of the Objective Law Itself*

It is not possible to define the attitude of the priest so precisely when he is faced with the rejection of *generally admitted* divine or ecclesiastical *laws* or with clearly obliging positive laws, and when his efforts to bring about a better insight fail completely. May he, in such circumstances, respect the decision of conscience of the believer, or must he draw the conclusion that he is faced with obvious bad faith on the part of somebody who claims to be a Christian and at the same time wants to escape the most undeniable obligations of his Christian state?

A solution might perhaps be found in reinterpretation of a concept often used by classic moral theology, that of invincible error. This meant ignorance or error concerning the law which cannot be removed even by a careful investigation proportioned to the importance of the case, either because the case is too complicated, or because no unambiguous solution appears to be possible, or because the person in question has insufficient intellectual or spiritual development at his disposal. It was quite generally admitted that this error did not excuse in the case of the elementary obligations of the natural law and that it certainly could no longer be maintained once the person had been sufficiently instructed about the law and its obligatory character. Classic moral theology would have deemed it absurd that a priest should invoke this concept of invincible error in order to consider as a decision of conscience made in good faith the rejection by a cultivated person of clearly known divine or ecclesiastical laws.

Yet should we not *considerably broaden* the concept of "ignorance" and "error" in the light of modern discoveries with regard to the lack of freedom in man's actions? With the whole of modern psychology we may safely accept as true that man never grasps things in their pure objectivity, that he always has an *"imago"* of them—that is, a mixture of objective data with all kinds of subjective pre-judgments, projected out of the unconscious onto things. Man looks at everything through the spectacles of his total psychological state of mind and of his past. It is not within his power to lay down these glasses, any more than it is possible for others to take them away from him. Man does not see the priest, but "his" image of the priest, not the Church, but his image of the Church, not the law but his vision of the law. The best arguments will often glance off that image without endangering the good faith of the person in question.

Hence the notion of invincible error cannot be restricted to a lack of material information or of a rational grasp of that information; it must be extended to the whole sphere of psychological incomprehension, unconscious resistance, invincible prejudices, wishful thinking and affective transferences of every kind. To claim that these unconscious deformations of reality cannot normally affect the meaning of the global judgment is a very handy formula, but it is one which in domains other than that of morality—politics, art, human sympathy and antipathy—is often contradicted by the facts. Everybody knows the type of the fanatical politician, of the forever deceived yet hopeful lover, of the scholar who is caught in his preconceived ideas. People shake their heads over them, but nobody will question their good faith, however disputable or even evidently senseless one may deem their position. Why should something similar not be possible for objectively evident moral problems?

What attitude should the priest assume before this stubbornly erring good faith? On the one hand he must continue to represent quietly but integrally the divine and ecclesiastical exigency in its *objectivity*. At no moment may he give the impression that the moral decision of his interlocutor can be objectively correct, or that it really does not matter much, that sincerity is the only thing that counts. On the other hand, he must always take very seriously the right of the erring *good faith,* and he may never question this good faith without serious reasons. Within the mutual tension of these two moments, a very supple yet very logical line of conduct takes shape, which allows one to keep up the *dialog* with the other and to give inner sincerity time to break through the prejudices and affective inhibitions and bring light. For the very fact that the visitor wishes to compare his dissenting decision with the opinion of the Church hints that his conviction is perhaps not as irreformable as he himself thinks.

There is one point, however, where the difficulty becomes very serious. The priest must resolutely cling to the objective truth. Does this imply that absolution should be denied, if it is requested? If we put the question in that way, it seems to falsify the perspective of the problem. For the problem concerns not the refusal of an absolution but rather the realization that it is senseless to ask for absolution in the situation at hand, and the exigency that the interlocutor should be logical with his own conscience. When the priest explains to him how it makes no sense to refuse the Church's mediation in ruling his conscience while yet asking that mediation to implore God's mercy, he should add at once that a direct contact with God in prayer and contrition remains possible, provided it involves the wish to accept again, as soon as this seems possible, the sacramental mediation of the Church. In this way refusing to hear the penitent's confession will avoid the semblance of haughty clerical condemnation; it will simply consist in noting a provisionally insoluble situation of conflict to which a solution must be found in the future, or at least earnestly sought after. Here too both moments, the ruthlessness of the objective truth and respect for the sincere subjectivity, are really reconciled.

Somebody tells the priest—to take at once an extreme example—"I can no longer in conscience perform my Easter duty nor go to Mass on Sundays. I do not really have the faith any more, and I should no longer be honest if I kept doing it." What attitude shall the priest assume?

The First Vatican Council condemned as heretical the assertion that the believer possesses the same right to doubt his faith as the unbeliever has to doubt his lack of faith or the follower of another religion to doubt his religion and to be converted to the Catholic Church. And indeed the inner attracting grace of God, which is at work in faith, makes the believer's situation totally different. This does not imply, however, that this inner light of grace will always penetrate sufficiently onto the plane of clear consciousness to prevent every error in good faith. There is no reason whatsoever not to apply to faith also the principle which is true for all virtues. In a note to the preparatory schema of Vatican I on faith, that possibility was explicitly mentioned, precisely in connection with invincible error: "It may happen accidentally (*per accidens*) and in certain circumstances that the conscience of a poorly educated Catholic will be led into such invincible error that he will adhere to a non-Catholic sect without becoming guilty of a formal sin against faith. In that event he would not have lost the faith and he would not be formally, but only materially, a heretic."[40] As we have already observed, the expression "poorly educated" should be extended, in the light of modern psychology, so that it may include not only intellectual limitations but also all other psychological deformations which may falsify the image of the Church and of the faith.

If the priest simply answers: "You must follow your conscience," he throws his interlocutor back into his unbelief as into a definite situation, and he is overlooking the assent to grace which continues, perhaps, to be present. Should the priest, on the other hand, answer: "One never has the right to give up one's faith," he crushes his visitor under the objective weight of the truth, and he seems to be questioning his good faith without any acceptable reason. But he may also answer: "If I understand you correctly, you are facing such doubts and difficulties that your inner Yes to God can no longer recognize itself in the Church. Therefore you must act logically according to your conscience. But this situation might be temporary. It is possible that your inner fidelity to God may again, sooner or later, recognize itself in the Church. Hence in order to keep faith with your conscience, you must go on searching and keep yourself open for every new breakthrough of the light." That answer is more complete than the two previous ones and theologically more correct. It takes the whole objective reality into account, yet it exerts not the slightest coercion on the subjective sincerity. It will often be the starting point for a dialog carried on in full freedom, whereby time is gained for the crisis to reach a solution from within.

The situation is quite different again if it is not a mature, but an *immature conscience* which is in collision with the law.

In that case the resistance to the law will generally be only a symptom of a deeper-lying question about the meaning of things or a clumsy effort to reach adulthood without paying the costs. Quietly ignoring the symptom, the priest will look for the real problems and try to solve them by helping his penitent to reach real adulthood.

In each of the foregoing cases we have been concerned with a dissenting decision of conscience in a member of the laity.

How about the case where the *priest's* own conscience enters
into conflict with the law? For the priest too—even more than
the rest of the faithful, owing to his scientific study of moral
theology or his experience as a spiritual guide—can reach new
insights about certain laws and unusual interpretations for
them. He too may, through circumstances, get caught in a
crisis and fall into invincible error in good faith concerning
specific points of divine or ecclesiastical moral doctrine. What
should be his attitude in such cases?

In the *confessional* the priest is the representative of the
Church. The faithful are very much aware of this, and the
fact that the validity of the sacrament depends on the facul-
ties he has juridically received allows of no doubt on this
point. He must judge of the applicability of the law in every
single instance according to the insights of his own conscience.
The jurisdiction he has received shows that the Church trusts
his maturity and competence in these matters. However, if his
interpretation of the law itself should dissent from the positions generally admitted in the Church, he has no right to
follow that personal opinion as norm for his conduct in the
confessional. He must give his penitent the answer which the
latter expects from him, the answer of the Church.

Outside of confession the priest is entitled to his own opinion and is allowed to defend it, with the necessary discretion.
He should, however, be aware that even people who consult
him outside of confession want not so much to hear his own
opinion as to know what the Church thinks of the question
at hand. Hence it would not be honest if he did not take that
wish into account but offered his own dissenting opinion
without pointing out that it was a new opinion, covered by
no other guarantee than his own thoughtfulness and competence. Moreover, it would be irresponsible to oppose one's

own opinion to an interpretation of the law generally admitted
in the Church without having compared that opinion with that
of competent people and tested it in serious discussion.

A fortiori it is unacceptable that a priest, in or outside of
confession, in his capacity as a religious guide, should assume
a *negative attitude* with respect to objective divine or ecclesiastical laws with which he can no longer agree. If he is convinced in good faith that honesty of conscience no longer
allows him to accept certain laws, the same honesty will force
him to function no longer as the representative of a Church
of which he rejects some essential positions. In such a case
his honesty of conscience will make him ask his superiors to
free him, at least for a time, of those tasks in which his
conscience would conflict with his function in the Church.

Nowhere, perhaps, has the opposition between law and love
been so sharply drawn as by Dostoyevski,[41] when the Great
Inquisitor faces Christ, whom he has jailed and is now examining. "You have come to bring love to man," says the Great
Inquisitor, "but we have seen that man cannot bear the liberty
of love, we have safely put him back under the yoke of the
law, and we shall not tolerate your throwing him into any
more adventures." The prisoner does not answer, but suddenly
he advances towards the Great Inquisitor and kisses his blood-
less lips. No compromise appears to be possible. The law
stubbornly remains law, aiming to protect and to shelter.
Love remains love, with its own uncanny logic. There can
be no doubt which side Dostoyevski is on. Neither can it be
doubted that many of our contemporaries consider his choice
as prophetic for the option of our time.

Yet our time is also wondering whether the strong law-love
opposition is not a moment of antithesis, unavoidable after
centuries in which the two were slavishly identified, to be in

its turn transcended in a final synthesis. Would a synthesis not be available for these many seekers—if not a systematic, at least an existential synthesis—in the prophetic figure of John XXIII, in whom no hint of a revolutionary spirit or of rebelliousness against the law was ever visible, and who nevertheless rose above all narrow legalism with the royal freedom and simplicity of one who was in the grasp of Christ's love?

4

The Mystique of Sin

"Ethics is a crust which renders man proof against grace."
That quip of Péguy's strikes very precisely the third dominant
note of the modified sense of sin, one which still remains to
be considered. It is no longer a question of human action in
its freedom or lack of freedom; here we are concerned with
the relation between the moral and the religious sense of sin.
Adopting the term first used by Karl Rahner for this phenomenon, we may speak of a tendency on the part of the
modern consciousness towards a "mystique of sin."[42]

THE PROBLEM

When, in the first chapter, we made a distinction between
the moral and religious levels of the ethical domain, we took
it for granted that the latter was a prolongation of the former
and that the whole of our moral striving was assumed by the
religious level, according to the general principle that grace
builds on nature.

The *mystique of sin* rejects that hypothesis. Instead of
emphasizing the continuity between moral and religious
ethics, it puts the accent very strongly upon their mutual
opposition. Accordingly, there is no such thing as natural

morality, and within the sin-grace tension in which man's
whole existence actually has its course, what one would like
to call natural ethics in fact stands on the side of sin. Man
must be saved even from being moral, if he really wants to
stand open for grace. What we call moral rectitude is in
reality always anthropocentrically referred to self, it is self-
respect, self-development, self-confidence. Hence it is always
smugness, the conviction that one can stand before God by
one's own strength and that one may demand acknowledgement and respect from him. In fine, all that Jesus has so ruthlessly combated in the Pharisees and Paul considers as the
exact opposite of salvation: "For by grace you have been
saved through faith: and that not from yourselves, for it is
the gift of God; not as the outcome of works, lest anyone may
boast" (Eph. 2.8–10).

Only one thing can save us from this pharisaism: the
experience of sin which shakes us out of our security, our
self-possession, our self-centered complacency. Only this reveals to us our real situation before God and lays us open,
through the experience of our need for redemption, to the
merciful bestowal of his grace. Holiness which has not passed
through the experience of sin cannot help ending up in
pharisaism. It is all too tempting for man to believe in his own
self-sufficiency. And in relation to his sinful fellow man, one
convinced of his own righteousness will necessarily remain a
useless and haughty stranger, instead of attesting, and helping
his fellow man to share, the mercy and the undeserved salvation he has himself experienced.

Even when we have been saved, we are still sinners, constantly standing in need of the grace of God's forgiveness.
"If we say that we have no sin, we deceive ourselves, and the
truth is not in us" (1 Jn. 1.8). Only then are we real Chris-

tians: people who sin, who acknowledge it, and who by so doing allow the mercy and overwhelming grace of God to make itself fully felt. The Christian's only hope lies not in the sanctuary of innocence but in constantly failing, in the constantly renewed disappointment of infidelity and sinfulness whereby we first become aware of our real religious situation. Hence avoiding sin or overcoming it by moral effort does not matter much. What does chiefly matter is to know in faith and hopeful confidence that in spite of our sin we are always enveloped in the all-forgiving grace of the Lord.

As can be seen, such a theory comes very close to the Protestant vision of the relation between sin and grace, with its assertion of the total depravity of human life resulting from original sin, the irresistible force of concupiscence and the mere imputation of justice whereby the Christian remains radically a sinner throughout his whole life. That is why one cannot find a systematic presentation of it in the work of any Catholic theologian, except as a refutation and a warning against it. Nevertheless, it has penetrated into Catholic *mentality* as a spontaneous resonance—not theologically clarified and hence not refutable—of a whole family of novels in which it is the mainspring of the action in the form of an unexpressed presupposition.

Thus in *Luise Rinser's* novel *Daniela* we meet with an undisguised example of the mystique of sin. Daniela comes as a teacher to a village whose inhabitants live in exterior, and even more in interior, moral wretchedness. How can one help them? Others have tried and failed. A young clergyman, too, is exerting his best efforts. But the townspeople shut themselves off, inaccessible to all help from people who are living in another spiritual climate far removed from the sinfulness in which they are trapped. Might they not be raised out of their humiliation if their helpers too turned sinful, thus entering their world? The author develops this temptation, to which Daniela and the priest succumb. The guilt of that sin and its subsequent expiation lead to a change of heart on the part of these people, and thus save them. Sin is presented as an effect of God's grace (p. 298) and the woman as an instrument of that grace (p. 300). The author concludes explicitly: "One should sin like these people. As long as one does not live their life and sin as they do, one cannot help them."[43] The novels of *Graham Greene*, too, have fostered a sympathy for sin mystique in many readers, not so much because their heroes are living in that mystique, but rather because he so systematically deals with extreme cases that this exclusive preference itself gives these cases some kind of normative meaning.

ELEMENTS OF A SOLUTION

It cannot be denied that this mystique of sin sounds like something profoundly and authentically Christian. All the same one has a feeling that somewhere along the line that real spirituality, under some slight, unnoticed push, has lost its true direction. Somewhere someone has played false with a very deep religious value. Where exactly?

All teachers of the spiritual life emphasize the truth that our moral effort, caught up as it is within the antagonism between sin and grace, can also be threatened by sin and drawn into the sphere of its influence. In each one of us there lives a *Pharisee*, and the merciless earnestness with which Christ rebuked pharisaical smugness contains for us also an ever actual warning. Especially since the Christian pharisee has read the parables, he has learned to vest his pharisee's prayer in the publican's formulas, and his "pride and vain-glory are sitting vainly at the lower end of the table, the same pride and vainglory as formerly, nay worse ones."[44] This does not mean, however, that all moral effort must necessarily arise from pharisaical pride of self and degenerate inevitably into sinfulness. That is a specifically Protestant view which the Catholic sense of faith rejects. Grace does not spare us our moral effort; on the contrary, that moral effort itself shares in the redemption, is brought to the healing of humility and raised to self-donation by grace.

It is true that in fact the healing process very often begins with the concrete experience of sin. Generally it is only when every support in his own being falls away that man consents to abandon his reliance on self and to appeal to God in a liberating "Thou." Frequently the brutal, humiliating shock of sin is for a man the only way out of the illusion of his complacency and of the myth carefully nurtured by social conventions of his respectability and decency. But it is not the mere fact of sin which produces this shock, but the shattering impact of that fact on the illusion of virtue and irreproachability in which he was living and the ensuing *awareness of sin*. An awareness of sin which is at the same time the awareness of his own dereliction, the experience of his inability to stand before God by his own power, the sense of his sinful involvement with the evil of the whole of humanity in which he is trapped, and the realization of his utter unworthiness to be loved by God. At the exact moment when he sins that awareness cannot be present, it would make sin impossible. Only detested sin, sin redressed by contrition, can feed that awareness and transform it into a conscious need for salvation and a welcoming of grace. Only in that sense can the liturgy speak of a *"felix culpa"* and Augustine paraphrase the words of Paul, that "for those who love God everything works unto good, even sin."

Hence it is absurd to think that sin as an *actual reality* will automatically have a redemptive value or that the actual experience of sin is indispensable if one is to arrive at this awareness of sin. Exactly the opposite is true: by its very definition sin, every sin, makes us blind to that awareness of sin. Whereas holiness, the rising out of sin into the love of God, opens our eyes more and more to our own unholiness and our need of redemption and makes us experience that rising out of sin more and more as mercy and undeserved grace. That a man begins to feel himself more of a sinner as he commits fewer sins is not based upon a pious exaggeration or illusion. It only demonstrates that sin is the lowest stage in a process of experiencing his distance from God and his unholiness in the presence of God's love which in the saint turns into a kind of despair over his inability to possess God in a more undivided way. But this is an accepted despair which involves a total expropriation of self and a complete submersion, in the midst of one's own helplessness, in the saving and sanctifying mercy of God. Thus no one has been more deeply aware of the need for redemption, no one further removed from every kind of pharisaical pride, than Mary, who was wholly without sin. Precisely because of her spotless purity she was the most completely surrendered to God and became likewise the most fully understanding of all human dereliction, the "refuge of sinners."

It is *a fortiori* unwarranted to suppose that a *voluntary seeking* of, or even a passive yielding to, sin might even in the slightest way contribute to the awakening of an authentic awareness of sin. Viewing the matter from the standpoint of God's eternal, all-knowing providence, we are able to understand how God can see, even in the sin itself, the change of heart it will bring about; how for him that sin, already at the moment in which it is committed, can be a *felix culpa* and one moment in a process of growth. But man's willing is done in time, and he is unable to unify for himself, in some kind of *prevenient self-mercy*, what is unified in God's merciful providence. God can already, in the sinner, love the future convert; but a man cannot, at the same time as he loves his sin, will his conversion. It is authentically Christian for man to trust in a God who can write straight even with man's crooked lines, but deliberately to write with crooked lines in order to see at work God's art of writing straight is to debase God's merciful love into a splendid toy for a spoiled child of man. The living God will not be mocked. Not man, but he alone is the Lord, also and especially in his mercy. At once we understand why the mystique of sin makes such a disagreeable impression. It robs a deeply religious moment of its real meaning and turns it into self-flattery and self-indulgence. Something that aims to present itself as the highest religious maturity is in reality a typical expression of religious infantilism. What claims to be self-donation, for better or for worse, to the living God turns out to be narcissistic self-spoiling with the help of a toy God.

It may be that a man's marital infidelity will give rise to a crisis resolved by him and his wife in a new discovery of each other and a renewal of love between them; later on, as the occasion of a new breakthrough, his sin may be assumed into their mutual love. It is even possible that the unhappy wife, when she sees the infidelity coming on, may also suspect that it will become an opportunity for a new breakthrough. She may then, as it were, accept and love by anticipation the liberating effect of her husband's sin, although her pain and disappointment will not grow any less for that reason. But the husband who would deliberately be unfaithful to his wife in order to know the splendor of a later reconciliation and the wholly new taste of a recovered love would only manifest an appalling infantile perversion.

That a priest and a woman should yield to their human attraction for each other, that out of the desperate struggle to grow into a real love through and across their sin they should reach a wholly new acquaintance with the need of the souls entrusted to their care and a bodily sense of authenticity in the preaching of God's mercy, is a wholly tenable theme, and Hawthorne brought it to life more than a century ago in his *Scarlet Letter*. But that they should, as in Rinser's novel, deliberately experiment with sin as with a new method of apostolic work—that is in both the human and the religious sense wholly incredible and false.

The same Paul who says: "Where the offense has abounded, grace has abounded yet more" also asks: "Shall we continue in sin that grace may abound? By no means!" (Rom. 5.20; 6.1). And the same John who says: "If we say that we have no sin, we deceive ourselves, and the truth is not in us," adds a little further on: "And by this we can be sure that we know God, if we keep his commandments. He who says that he knows him, and does not keep his commandments, is a liar and the truth is not in him. But he who keeps his word, in him the love of God is truly perfected; and by this we know that we are in him. He who says that he abides in him, ought himself also to walk just as he walked." (1 Jn. 1.8; 2.3–6) And what would the Lord, who pours scorn on the Pharisees so mercilessly, have said, if a publican who had heard his parable had prayed as follows in the temple: "I thank thee, Lord, because again and again I commit sins and because on that account I am so much better than yonder Pharisee. For I at least shall go home justified, and he will not." Does the mystique of sin not come dangerously close to the "pharisaism of the publican"? A less expensive pharisaism even than that of the Bible, one that does not even pay God off with tithes and fasting, but wishes to buy his grace only with its sins.

APPLICATIONS ON THE PASTORAL LEVEL

The mystique of sin expresses itself in a certain mentality, in the point of view from which judgments are made, more than in specific practices. Hence pastoral care will have to turn its attention to that mentality in order to hold the right middle position between pharisaism and the mystique of the publican.

AUTHENTIC AND UNAUTHENTIC INNOCENCE

A primary domain in which modern Christian opinion is badly in need of clarification involves the concepts of "innocence" and "wholeness." Considerable ambiguity is manifested in the use and evaluation of these ideas, for they too may be understood on the three levels of signification mentioned in our first chapter.

There is a taboo innocence, consisting in the fact of being undamaged, inviolate; it is supposed to be present in the child as a matter of course, and it is destroyed by certain events. The child is supposed to be a *tabula rasa*, a void, in which the passions and instincts of the adult are not as yet present, but into which they may be introduced from without. The young being "to whom nothing has happened yet" is innocent. And this happening refers, of course, mainly to the sexual sphere, in which the strongest taboos prevail. The boy who, unaware perhaps of the meaning of his action, masturbates for the first time, "loses" his innocence, and the psychopath who rapes a girl "robs her of her innocence."

There is also a *moral innocence,* which might better be called *wholeness,* or *integrity.* It depends not so much on what one has *gone through* as on the manner in which these experiences have been assimilated—in other words, on what one has *become* through them. Decisive here is not the absence of any risks, but the manner in which these risks have been assumed. Someone may have gone through all kinds of experiences of guilt. Provided he has integrated them, out of his inner freedom, in such a way that ultimately he possesses himself harmoniously in a totally conscious way, that person is morally a whole (or sound) person, even though from the taboo point of view he may be far from innocent. Is the child in this moral sense sounder and more innocent than the adult? Perhaps. But only because generally evil has not yet affected the child's inner freedom, since he is still more undivided than the adult, willing the good with greater spontaneity and harmony, even though he already carries within himself all the germs of division and inner cleavage. When Christ proposes the child's innocence as an example and has such stern words for those who scandalize children, he means that soundness, not taboo innocence.

Finally, there is a *religious wholeness and innocence* which is entirely determined by one's relation to God's merciful love. For this wholeness sin has meaning only insofar as it is a screen which cuts off divine love. Forgiveness makes man a new creature. Sin overcome in contrition becomes a moment of growth in the new wholeness, it becomes an organic element of a restoration more marvelous—*mirabilius reformasti—*

than the original project. Only from one point of view that wholeness remains imperfect, owing to what Catholic theology calls "temporal punishments," to be suffered even after the forgiveness of sin. In fact they are the person himself and the surrounding world of men and of things as they have been sullied and deformed by sin. But where the return to God in contrition is deepest, precisely there it exerts a creative and transforming influence on human reality, so that even this historical defilement is restored in a new history and transformed into a lovelier growth. For man's past is not a self-contained, finished reality. It is caught up in the totality of his duration, and each new decision and change transforms all that is past by giving it a new meaning and a new direction. From the religious point of view Mary Magdalene is undeniably a "whole" woman, not in spite of her past but partially because of it. Charles de Foucauld, himself a convert, has realized this very vividly. His special devotion to her by no means derived from the fact that she also had come to Christ out of sin, but only from the fact that, after Mary his mother, no woman had been more loved by Christ than she. From the moral point of view one may say that Mary Magdalene is a woman who has recovered a fine integrity. From the point of view of taboo she remains, even as a convert, a fallen woman, and one may wonder why Christ let her come near him.

The extent to which a mere taboo-conception of innocence is rejected by Jesus is evident not only from his attitude towards Mary Magdalene. In the parable of the prodigal son it is obvious, too, that the elder son, although he has always stayed "in the house," has never, like the younger son, really come "home." Hence, despite his self-asserted taboo innocence, he is irrevocably more lost than his younger brother.

Most of Jesus' reproaches for the Pharisees are aimed at their overevaluation of outer performances and at their cult of merely social legal virtues.[45]

It is a fact that during the last two centuries Christian thought has put the *accent* very heavily on *taboo innocence;* indeed to such an extent that many have identified it, almost without further ado, with Christian wholeness. There is quite a bit of pharisaism involved in this confusion of ideas.

It is normal and wholesome that the adult, who has already to a great extent written his life, when he considers his own divided unauthenticity, all his lost opportunities, his disappointments and irreparable deformations, should conceive an intense nostalgia for the unwritten book of the child's life as for a *paradise lost.* But this is also a very complex feeling, in which all kinds of components of very different origin and value work together.

It comprises the realization of the vulnerableness and frailty of all that is in its springtime and first beginnings, the realization also of the decisive importance a deviation or a wrong orientation at the start can have for all further growth and, associated with it, a sense of responsibility and a desire to protect a being so frail and so important. That insight conforms with the mercilessly stern words of Jesus about scandal given to children. Even deeper, perhaps, lies the awareness of an image of all that is human damaged in the beginning, and the desire to be saved from this inner hereditary cleavage and restored to the original integrity. It is to this deepest yearning that Jesus appeals in giving himself the name "Son of man," which Paul makes explicit in the image of the "new Adam" and in the whole theology of redemption built on it.

But equally present in that nostalgia is the unexpressed longing for the liberty of a still unhindered, impersonal yielding to instinctive life, a child's dream world restricted by no moral consciousness, by no concrete vital choice—the paradise of innocence of a being in possession of all human possibilities without any human responsibilities, somewhere beyond good and evil. And further, all the personally unsatisfied needs for tenderness and self-coddling are unconsciously projected in this nostalgia for childhood, the wish also to satisfy one's own need for affection by possessing and enjoying the malleable mind of the child.

The myths of the paradise lost and regained and of the golden age, with the child of man as an archetypal symbol of lost perfection, illustrate in a striking way the *ambiguity* of this nostalgia. Characteristically, in the works of contemporary literature in which this mythical theme is revived, the ethical and religious dimensions are frequently ignored or kept vague (the relative authenticity of the "Little Prince" is rather exceptional), whereas there is a tendency towards a pseudo-paradisical happiness whose perversity is only veiled by poetical and aesthetic adornments.*

If, as is happening nowadays, that nostalgia for paradise is integrally raised to the status of a basic moral and theo-

---

* Jean Daniélou treats the theme of the nostalgia for paradise very suggestively in its several components. See "Les trois paradis" in *Culture et mystère* (Paris, 1948), pp. 46–73. He takes the distinction of the three possible solutions for that nostalgia—aesthetic, ethical and mystical—from Kierkegaard's *The Concept of Dread* (Princeton, 1917). In modern literature he refers to Alain-Fournier, Colette, Gide, Giraudoux, Proust, Péguy, Rilke. A sharp satire on modern pseudo-paradisical longing and amoral innocence may be found in the story of her conversion by F. Mallet-Joris, *Lettre à moi-même* (Paris, 1963), pp. 66–69.

logical value, its ambiguity will have effects on our whole moral attitude.

Everything then is attuned to the design of *preserving* that ideal childlike innocence as long as possible. The main purpose of education is to exclude as far as possible, or postpone as long as possible, all that endangers that innocence. Anxiety and overprotectiveness are promoted to Christian virtues. One feels like reproaching the father of the prodigal son for ever letting the youth go. The whole social attitude towards the sinner is dominated by defense reflexes, haunted by the idea of the scriptural millstone. This is exemplified in the inhuman treatment of unmarried mothers, in the social ostracism of a divorced relative or of the priest who has given up his calling; in the systematic rousing of suspicion against people of other faiths, in the ghetto mentality within which the faithful are locked up. All this is directly related to the naive glorification of childlike taboo innocence. Equating every considerable risk with a proximate occasion of sin derives to a great extent from the same misconception. The jealous resentment, too, of many an adult, who has remained "innocent," of the converted sinner who, "having had all the fun," will ultimately be saved all the same, harks back to the most primitive anxiety-innocence and taboo rebellion.

Thus being childlike unintentionally becomes synonymous with being childish or hypocritical, and a religion which proposes that childishness as an ideal is treated with the same kind of compassionate and suspicious smile as that with which a man of experience looks down on an "ingénue." Authentic childlikeness has acquired such a bad reputation on account of this ambiguity that there are Catholic philosophers and psychologists who, without further inquiry, heap scorn upon the "little way" of Thérèse of Lisieux and call it infantilism,* or even have a manifest grudge against our Lord's utterances about the need of becoming a child in order to enter the Kingdom.

THE GOOD SINNER

Contemporary man needs not only an exact idea of what innocence is, but also a more correct evaluation of his *situation as a sinner* within a Church of sinners. Once more, only the adult realization of sin on a specifically Christian-religious level will allow him to find the right middle position between accepting and rejecting his sinfulness. For if the mystique of sin puts acceptance too exclusively above rejection, it is only a reaction to a struggle against sin which includes an unchristian rejection of man's situation as a sinner, since it carries out that struggle from a taboo, or from a merely humanistic, standpoint.

To put the problem clearly, it is best to start with the person who is totally *in the grip* of sin. As long as temptation and

---

* In *Illusion and Anxiety* (New York, Macmillan, 1963) Marc Oraison explains the difference between spiritual childhood and infantilism through the example of the Little Flower. Starting from an affectivity which had been fixated on an infantile level by her environment, Thérèse, in the course of a few years, reaches a spiritual maturity which obviously lies beyond the reach of what may be explained by a purely human development, and this without any well-adapted psychological treatment or insight. The whole biography of Thérèse of Lisieux by Ida Görres, *The Hidden Face* (New York, 1959), develops the opposition between the influence of the environment and the inner growth of the saint. See also L. Beirnaert, "Enfance spirituelle et infantilisme," in *Expérience chrétienne et psychologie* (Paris, 1964), pp. 143–154.

sin seem like passing, almost accidental, episodes in a man's life, he is able to ignore his sinful condition to the extent of not being forced to take a definite stand on it. But when he is wholly engulfed by evil, when every moral recovery is followed so quickly by a new fall that he no longer sees any way out; when his own past harasses him; when circumstances put him permanently into a situation he is not equal to or demand a heroism of which he is incapable: only then does he come face to face with his sinful existence in such a way that he must find some means of synthesizing his acceptance and rejection of sin.

If he is a person still at the *taboo level* of morality, he is utterly unable to accept his sinfulness—least of all before God, who is then the supreme threat, in whose sight he feels pilloried in naked ugliness. The only solution then is to shake off the awareness of his sinfulness to some extent by comparing himself with others, by hiding, as it were, behind their still greater sinfulness, to divert God's scrutinizing gaze towards their more conspicuous deformity. Through this comparison with others he also diverts his own attention from God. He builds a protecting wall between himself and God with the sins of the others, so that he really no longer has to stand before him. That is what the Pharisee did in the parable. Man is really aware of being a sinner only when he stands before God in his naked poverty, like the publican, who, as Kierkegaard noted, "had not even seen that there was a Pharisee in the temple." But then taboo will no longer suffice, then the taboo attitude means despair without any way out. That is why the taboo-motivated person runs away, even though he acknowledges his sinfulness in words. Just as the unjust creditor could give his master the impression that he really acknowledged his debt, whereas it was all too evident from his attitude towards his fellow servant that he was merely using a formula to stave off the impending punishment. His cruel harshness may have been mainly a means of "saving face" by taking revenge for the humiliation he had just suffered.

One meets this flight mechanism regularly in the psychology of the *criminal*. He fixes his attention so completely on his own claims and his strictures on his fellow men, society and the existing situation, that he becomes totally blind with regard to the value of his own actions and settles down into the conviction that the crime committed or to be committed is wholly justified. Only when he meets love, which makes him cease the infantile taboo resistance, is he able to admit his own guilt, to make it good and overcome it. We observe this frequently in the criminals described in world literature. Raskolnikov remains obdurate in his proud self-sufficiency until he is overcome by Sonja's selfless love; the pickpocket of Bresson's film has a change of heart only under the influence of the equally selfless love of his girl friend, Jeanne.

Among *"petty" sinners* too the same escape mechanism operates, mostly under the guise of losing oneself anonymously in the universal sinfulness—"Everybody does it"; "There is no way of getting out of it"; "What can you do about it? we are that way in our family"; "We are young, and we live only once." Very useful reasons for minimizing one's own guilt are also found today in psychology; in our time a psychological excuse is considered the most universally human, and any motive universally accepted as valid is deemed the best. Even religious-sounding expressions may hide an attempt to escape.

"Well, we are all sinners," or "That is the way man is" all too often means: "I need not be ashamed, for we are all in the same boat."

With all its exaggerations, the mystique of sin has perhaps the advantage that it ruthlessly jolts the Christian out of this pharisaical taboo illusion and teaches him to see the religious acceptance of his sinfulness as the only way out of the dilemma: despair or flight from God.

Nor will *moral honesty* suffice for man to reach a real admission of his sinful condition—at least, not if he does not go beyond it, but reduces religious self-donation to moral steadiness in the good. "With the help of grace," a man adds; but that grace is seen mainly as a strengthening of his own power of self-control and self-conquest. When one who has striven for this merely moral equilibrium is confronted with the experience of his own helplessness, of constantly repeated falls and yielding to evil, he can only feel himself a failure before God.

There is no longer any refuge in flight, because God is in the conscience itself. Comparing oneself with *others* is of no avail, for the image of one's own failure mirrored in the failure of others fully reveals the depth to which one has fallen, and comparison with successful persons only deepens the impression of one's own deficiency. From *God* himself man may expect no direct help, for the God of ethics always refers a man to his own conscience, for which evil can be undone only through the person's own endeavors. Therefore, when what has been painfully rebuilt is again and again brought down by man's own weakness, all that remains to him is to acknowledge his failure without any possibility of deliverance, in a remorselessly sincere but bitter admission of the sterility of his efforts, without offering any extenuating circumstances or excuses, in a kind of stoical pride—what Augustine called *superba dejectio* (proud dejection).

This condition expresses itself mainly in two ways. One way is: "I 'honestly' *acquiesce in my helplessness* and mercilessly draw the conclusions from it. If I cannot hold out in the sight of God, there is no sense in making believe. No more confession, for I cannot sincerely promise amendment. No more prayer or efforts to help others spiritually, for I cannot at the same time say Yes and No to God." Such an attitude is more common than one would suppose. Many people are not far from saying: "I must first have conquered my sins before I go to confession again. I must reform my life before I can enter into contact with God through prayer again." They do not realize that this attitude is diametrically opposed to the meaning of confession and prayer. They cannot realize it, because they have reduced the religious love dialog with God to some kind of moral self-respect.

In others discouragement turns sooner or later into *rebellion*. They turn away in bitterness from a God who does not grant them the strength to do what he asks of them.

Here too the mystique of sin touches upon a real shortcoming in the attitude of many Christians. It rightly points out the blind alley one enters when the thing love asks of us is made into an urge for performances. The all too self-directed impetuosity with which a man struggles with sin makes him unable to rise out of it.

Thus only an authentically *Christian-religious* evaluation of his own situation can bring man to accept the fact that he is a sinner; such an acceptance does not hinder but promotes the fight against evil.

At first glance it would seem that his own sinfulness should be even *more unbearable* for the religious person than for the ethical person. For nothing is harder to bear than to live continually in the presence of a love to which one has been unfaithful. In one of his novels Mauriac has described the awful situation—worse than death—of a woman who, driven by frustration and despair, has attempted to murder her husband, and who feels condemned to spend her whole life, without hope of release, in the presence of this man. He knows, but he does not understand and will never forgive. Is hell anything but a clinging to sin in the presence of an inescapable, eternally immutable love? How can a man conjure that horror away?

Only by *reversing* the relationship, by converting his sin from the refusal it is into a consent to love; by yielding everything, including his sin, to the love which demands all. This is the only possible solution; but it is also the radical, all-renewing, creative one. Instead of fleeing *from* God—a foredoomed attempt—fleeing *into* God; offering one's very sinfulness in the supreme boldness of trust: "I am so sure of thy love that I dare to come to thee even with my unfaithfulness; thou art able to love even my infidelity."[46]

In this way I may permanently unite, in an authentic balance of tension, without any spasmodic efforts and without self-delusion, the quiet acceptance of my sinfulness and the earnest of my endeavor to free myself from sin. A quiet *acceptance*, because I know that every new weakness is sheltered in the unconditional love of a God who, even when my heart accuses me, remains forever greater than my heart. The earnest of my *endeavor*: because that love remains at every moment all-demanding and can be an unconditional possibility of sheltering mercy for me only if I acknowledge that it is all-demanding. The two moments converge into Christian *hope*.

Even if my powers keep forever failing, I do not despair of myself; I cannot despair, because God keeps relying on me and I may always rely on him, I may at every moment return home to him. The lost drachma retains his effigy, and the straying sheep bears his brand and knows his voice.

Even comparing myself with *others* can no longer disturb me in the acceptance of my sinfulness. For that sinfulness is experienced within a Holy Church which is a Church of sinners. I share with all Christians the humility with which all of us together stand before God as sinners. With all of them I share the prayer and intercession of the communion of saints for *"us sinners,"* as the prayers of the liturgy and the simple Hail Mary say again and again. I do not have to fear the judgment of others as long as they are authentic Christians. For each one of them looks at me with the eyes of God, who has hope for me and who knows that at every moment my sinfulness may be transformed into love and holiness. And as for the pharisees, who deem themselves such good Christians with their unchristian judgment, for them, in the joy of God's mercy for a prodigal son come home, I can share my Father's pity for my jealous elder brother.

The superiority of the religious over the moral-ethical sense of sin has its purest expression in the combination of a much greater detestation of sin with an infinitely greater mildness with regard to the sinner. The morality of the Middle Ages may still have been steeped in barbarity, but the pledge of their Christian hope was uttered in the invocation of God's mercy engraved on the executioner's sword and the sincerity with which the judge asked the criminal he had just condemned to death to intercede for him before God.

Only this explains the paradox of the *Saints* who, as they entered the full reality of God's love and with growing gener-

osity allowed this love to burn every sin out of their lives, also
reached an ever more peaceful acceptance of their sinful past,
devoid of any hint of sterile remorse or of tormenting recollection. In one of the antiphons of the feast of Peter, the
Church sings: "Even if I should have to die with thee, I will
not deny thee" (Mt. 26.35). The overconfident words which
called forth Christ's rebuke and the prediction of the denial!
Now these words are addressed to Peter as a song of praise. Is
this not the acknowledgment of a restoration so re-creative
that these words are no longer an empty human boast but
have mercifully turned into God's simple, everlasting truth?
For Peter will die rather than betray his Master, and he will
forever remember his unfaithfulness as the occasion of a triumph of God's conquering love.

By Way of Conclusion

This book should not end with a conclusion but with a question. All three directions in which contemporary consciousness is looking for a renovation of the sense of sin: the dialog of freedom with determinism, the dialectic of the law and the situation, the relation between sin and holiness, lie open for very ambivalent possibilities. All three represent both a threat and a promise for an authentic sense of sin.

A *threat*. Each of these three directions has led into a contemporary heresy: psychologism, situationism, the sin mystique. But heresies are never merely errors. They always come from the one-sided emphasis of values which are in danger of being lost or of losing their authentic savor in an all too nicely balanced equilibrium of faith or of conscience. That is why heresies are not only a danger for the Church; they are also a warning, and may become a boon.

Today's heresies about sin offer the *promise* of a renewed realization of extremely important values. They constitute a warning against a pharisaical "decent people" Christianity which all too often hides behind a strict observance of the law and a stern condemnation of sin to escape the deeper demands of the living God. Thank heaven, it has become almost impos-

sible for today's Christian to rid himself of sin with a collection
of recipes or simple arithmetic. Sin is being thrust into his
consciousness once more in all its human complexity and religious seriousness.

Hence every one of us is confronted with a *choice*. If he
wants to avoid the impact of the new discoveries, he may do
so by clinging rigidly to the old conceptions. Or he may put
the new discoveries at the service of unauthenticity. Thus he
may distort the complexity of his free action into unaccount-
ability, or deform its spontaneity into arbitrariness; he may,
with the capriciousness of a spoiled child, reduce the seriousness of the dialog with God to a simple game. On the other
hand, should he, despite the heavy burden of his psychic con-
ditionings, agree to meet God's all-demanding invitation in
every situation with the sincerity of his free response, today's
intellectual atmosphere offers him a unique opportunity to transcend all pharisaism and every infantile taboo attitude and to
face that invitation with a more mature decision of conscience,
experiencing in Christian authenticity God's saving judgment
on his own sinfulness and the sinfulness of others.

Moreover, owing to the present world situation, every individual choice acquires a *suprapersonal* importance. The
whole of mankind is vividly aware of an irresistible growth
towards unity, of the solidarity of all men in a common destiny
from which there can be no withdrawal. Mankind as well as
the individual is facing a choice. Will its unity be that of mass
formation, levelling and robotizing individuals, making every
personality the slave of some anonymous form of common welfare? Or will it be amorization, a free commitment to the ever
more intimate centering of love on the ultimate focus which
is Christ? In his personal decision each one commits the others

and bears the responsibility of the decision of his time. Each one throws the weight of his conscience, light or heavy, on the scales of history in an exceptional hour, which might be the hour of the daimon but is also that of the Spirit.

Bibliographical Notes

1. General bibliography: P. Anciaux, *The Sacrament of Penance* (New York, Sheed and Ward, 1962); P. Galtier, *Sin and Penance* (London, 1932); H. Rondet, *The Theology of Sin* (Notre Dame, Ind., Fides, 1960); P. Riga, *Sin and Penance* (Milwaukee, Bruce, 1962); A. von Speyr, *Confession* (New York, 1964); J. Sheerin, *The Sacrament of Freedom: A Book on Confession* (Milwaukee, Bruce, 1961); J. Oesterreicher, *The Israel of God* (New York, Kenedy, 1961), ch. 2, "Sin, Pardon, Redemption"; M. Oraison, *Sin* (New York, Macmillan, 1962); Paul Palmer, *Sacraments and Forgiveness* (Westminster, Md., Newman, 1959) for source material; M. Scheler, "Repentance and Rebirth," in *On the Eternal in Man* (New York, Harper, 1960); P. Régnier, *Le sens du péché* (Paris, 1954); L. Monden, *Moraal zonder zonde?* (Bruges, 1955); H. Bacht, "Die Welt von heute und das Gespür für die Sünde," *Geist und Leben*, 31 (1958), 7–16; L. Jerphanion, "Philosophie du repentir," *Nouv. Rev. Théol.*, 81 (1959), 392–399; *id.*, *Théologie du péché* (Tournai, 1960); *id.*, *Pastorale du péché* (Tournai, 1961); M. Zundel, *Morale et mystique* (Bruges, 1962); H. van Lier, *Le nouvel âge* (Tournai, 1962), pp. 205–222; P. Delhaye, *La conscience morale du chrétien* (Tournai, 1964); R. W. Gleason, *The World to Come* (New York, Sheed and Ward, 1958), pp. 13–42; J. Foster, "The Scapegoat and the Underdog: Ancient and Modern Sense of Guilt, Sin and the Community of Man," *Life of the Spirit*, 16 (1962), 430–443; P. De Letter, "The Sense of the Sin," *Clergy Monthly*, 26 (1962), 77–88; R. O'Connell, "Sense of Sin in the Modern World," *Way*, 2 (1962), 3–18.

See also the special issues devoted to the problems of confession and awareness of sin by: *Seelsorge*, 1958, Heft 2; *La Maison-Dieu*, nos. 55–56 (1958); *Christus*, January 1959; *Paroisse et liturgie*, October 1962; *Lumière et Vie*, no. 70 (1964).

2. See on this topic: E. Des Places, art. "Péché," in *Suppl. Dict. de la Bible*, vol. vii (1962), cols. 407–480; F. Manthey, "Religion als Erlebnis des Heiligen und Unheiligen," in *Theol. und Glaube*, 1964, 22–31.

Specifically concerning the feeling and the awareness of guilt, see: P. Régamey, "Avertissement des profondeurs," *La Vie Spir.*, 94 (1956), 133–166; C. Baudouin and L. Beirnaert, art. "Culpabilité," in *Dict. de Spiritualité*, vol. ii., cols. 2632–2654; J. M. Hollenbach, "Schuldgefühl und seelische Gesundheit," *Geist und Leben*, 48 (1958), 17–24; W. Bitter et al., *Angst und Schuld in theologischer und psychotherapeutischer Sicht* (Stuttgart, 1959); C. Nodet, "Psychanalyse et culpabilité," in *Pastorale du péché* (Tournai, 1961), pp. 237–266; G. Condreau, *Angst und Schuld als Grundprobleme der Psychotherapie* (Bern, 1962); G. Zilboorg, *Psychoanalysis and Religion* (New York, Farrar, Straus, 1962); M. Eck, "L'éducation du sentiment de culpabilité," *Etudes*, 315 (1962), 330–342; P. Ricoeur, *Finitude et culpabilité* (Paris, 1962); F. Bourdeau, "La hantise d'être jugé," *La Vie Spir.*, 109 (1963), 716–726; D. Dunphy, "Guilt: Its Psychological Aspects and Moral Implications," *Priestly Studies*, 28 (1961), 2–28; C. F. Tageson, "Neurotic and Normal Guilt," *Way* (U.S.), 18 (1962), 39–47; E. O'Doherty, "Freedom, Responsibility and Guilt," *Studies*, 52 (1963), 363–372; A. Schneiders, *The Anarchy of Feeling* (New York, Sheed and Ward, 1963).

3. See *Le coupable est-il un malade ou un pécheur?* (Coll. "Convergences," Paris, 1950); M. Oraison, *Love or Constraint?* (New York, Kenedy, 1961); Y. Congar, "Sommes-nous vraiment assez libres?" in *Vaste monde, ma paroisse* (Ed. Témoignage chrétien, 1959), pp. 100–109; M. Nicet, B. This and J. Vinchon, *Drogues et tranquillisants* (Tournai, 1962); P. Chauchard, *Biologie et morale* (Tours, 1959); *Les conditions biologiques indispensables à la liberté de l'homme* (Colloque international de philosophie des sciences, Leiden, 1961), Brussels, 1963; *L'action de l'homme sur le psychisme humain* (Coll. "Convergences," Paris, 1963); L. Beirnaert, *Expérience chrétienne et psychologie* (Paris, 1964); R. O'Connell, "Com-

pulsive Act and Habitual Sin: Problem of the Habitual Masturbator," *Guild Cath. Psychiatr.*, 10 (1963), 42–47; G. Hagmaier and R. Gleason, *Counselling the Catholic* (New York, Sheed and Ward, 1959).

4. For a deeper study of the philosophical aspects of human freedom, see L. VanderKerken, *De goede mens en zijn gebreken* (Antwerp, 1957); J. de Finance, *Existence et Liberté* (Paris, 1955); L. Janssens, *Liberté de conscience et liberté religieuse* (Paris, 1964), pp. 77–170; J. Mouroux, *The Meaning of Man* (New York, Image, 1961), chs. 7 and 8; J. Donceel, *Philosophical Psychology* (New York, Sheed and Ward, 1960), chs. 17 and 18.

5. See the forthcoming book of P. Schoonenberg, *Man in Sin* (Notre Dame, Ind., 1965); C. Stockford, "Sin, Hell and Sacraments: Distinction of Mortal and Venial Sin," *Downside Review*, 81 (1963), 22–36.

6. See B. Häring, *The Law of Christ* (Westminster, Md., Newman, 1961).

7. See K. Rahner, "Forgotten Truths Concerning the Sacrament of Penance," in *Theological Investigations* (Baltimore, Taplinger, 1963), vol. ii, pp. 135–174; *id.*, "Beichtprobleme," in *Schiften zur Theologie* (Einsiedeln, 1956), vol. iii, pp. 227–245; *id.*, "Vom Sinn der häufigen Andachtsbeichte," *ibid.*, vol. iii, pp. 211–226; P. Anciaux, *The Sacrament of Penance* (New York, Sheed and Ward, 1962); A. Snoeck, *Confession and Psychoanalysis* (Westminster, Md., Newman, 1964); "Equipe sacerdotale de Saint-Séverin," *La Pénitence* (Bruges, 1958); C. Dumont, "La réconciliation avec l'Eglise et la nécessité de l'aveu sacramentel," *Nouv. Rev. Théol.*, 81 (1959), 577–597; P. Anciaux, "The Ecclesiastical Dimension of Penance," *Theology Digest*, 11 (1963), 33–38; O. Semmelroth, "Das Bussakrament als Gericht," *Scholastik*, 37 (1962), 530–549; *Problèmes du confesseur* (Coll. "Problèmes de la religieuse d'aujourd'hui," Paris, 1963); C. Jean-Nesmy, *Pratique de la confession* ("Cahiers de la Pierre-qui-Vire," Paris, 1963).

8. The brochure of P. Anciaux and R. Blomme *Rencontrer Dieu dans la confession* (Kasterlee [Belgium], 1963) is an attempt to establish the examination of conscience on the religious relationship and the movement which animates it.

9. Cf. "La Pénitence dans la liturgie," *La Maison-Dieu*, nos. 55 and 56 (1958); "Die liturgische Erneuerung des Bussakramentes,"

Herder-Korrespondenz, 1959, pp. 297–304; "Sinn und Möglichkeiten einer liturgischen Erneuerung des Bussakramentes," *Herder-Korrespondenz,* 1960, pp. 180–189; *La Pénitence est une célébration* (Coll. de pastorale liturgique no. 58, Bruges, 1963); P. Riga, "The Liturgy of Confession," *Cross and Crown,* 16 (1964), 134–141.

10. R. Hostie, *L'entretien pastoral* (Paris, 1963), with a bibliography on pp. 250 and 252–253; A. Godin, *La relation humaine dans le dialogue pastoral* (Bruges, 1963); L. Beirnaert, "A propos du dialogue pastoral," *Etudes,* 319 (1963), 260–266.

All these works apply to pastoral theology the principles of non-directive or client-centered therapy of C. R. Rogers, as set forth in his *Counseling and Psychotherapy* (Boston, Houghton, 1942) and *Client-centered Therapy* (Boston, Houghton, 1951). See also C. A. Curran, *Counseling in Catholic Life and Education* (New York, Macmillan, 1952); C. R. Rogers and M. Kinget, *Psychothérapie et relations humaines* (Louvain, 1962); S. Hiltner and L. G. Colston, *The Context of Pastoral Counseling* (Nashville, Tenn., Abingdon, 1961); many issues of *The Catholic Counselor* (New York, Catholic Guidance Council) and of *Pastoral Psychology* (Manhasset, New York).

11. Cf. J. Goldbrunner, *Holiness Is Wholeness* (New York, Pantheon, 1955); L. Beirnaert, "La sanctification dépend-elle du psychisme?" *Etudes,* 226 (1950), 58–65; reprinted in *Expérience chrétienne et psychologie* (Paris, 1964), pp. 133–142; J. Bernhart, "Heiligkeit und Krankheit," *Geist und Leben,* 40 (1950), 172–195.

12. Cf. L. Ligier, *Péché d'Adam et péché du monde* (2 vols., Paris, 1960–61); J. de Fraine, *Adam et son lignage. Etudes sur la notion de "personnalité corporative" dans la Bible* (Bruges, 1959); S. Lyonnet, "Le péché originel en Rom. 5.12," *Biblica,* 1960, 325–355; R. Troisfontaines, *I Do Not Die* (New York, Desclée, 1963), pp. 208–228; R. Prendergast, "The Supernatural Existential, Human Generation and Original Sin," *Downside Review,* 82 (1964), 1–24; P. Schoonenberg, *Man in Sin* (Notre Dame, Ind., in preparation).

13. J. Onimus, *Face au monde actuel* (Paris, 1962).

14. H. Bergson, *The Two Sources of Morality and Religion* (New York, Doubleday, 1956); to be compared with C. Odier, *Les deux sources, consciente et inconsciente, de la vie morale* (Neuchâtel, 1947). See also H. Gouhier, *Bergson et le Christ des évangiles* (Paris, 1962).

15. A. Hesnard, *L'univers morbide de la faute* (Paris, 1949); *id., Morale sans péché* (Paris, 1954). A critique of both books in L. Beirnaert, "La 'Morale sans péché' du Dr. A. Hesnard," *Etudes*, 284 (1955), 35–49 (reprinted in *Expérience chrétienne et psychologie*, pp. 261–280); P. Ricoeur, "Morale sans péché ou péché sans moralisme?" *Esprit*, 22 (1954), 294–312; *id.*, "Morale sans péché?" *Recherches et débats*, no. 11 (Paris, 1955). The quoted text in *Morale sans péché*, p. 165.

16. J.-P. Sartre, *Being and Nothingness* (New York, Knopf, 1956); *id., L'existentialisme est un humanisme* (Paris, 1946); *id., The Flies* (New York, Knopf, 1947); *id., The Devil and the Good Lord* (New York, Knopf, 1960); S. de Beauvoir, *The Ethics of Ambiguity* (New York, 1949); see also: E. Brisbois, "Le sartrisme et le problème moral," *Nouv. Rev. Théol.*, 74 (1952), 30–48 and 124–145.

17. F. Jeanson, *Le problème moral et la pensée de Sartre* (Paris, 1947); *id.*, "Les caractères existentialistes de la conduite humaine selon Jean-Paul Sartre," in *Morale chrétienne et requêtes contemporaines* (Tournai, 1954), pp. 173–194; G. Gusdorf, *Traité de l'existence morale* (Paris, 1950).

18. The International Humanist and Ethical Union (I.H.E.U.) has acquired a certain influence, especially in the Anglo-Saxon countries, in Scandinavia and in Benelux. See *Proceedings of the First International Congress on Humanism and Ethical Culture*, Utrecht, 1957; J. Huxley, *Man in the Modern World* (New York, New American Library, 1947); *id., Evolution in Action* (New York, Harper, 1953).

19. Cf., for instance, P. Teilhard de Chardin, *The Phenomenon of Man* (New York, Harper, 1959), pp. 254–267; *Christologie et évolution* (unpublished), 1933, pp. 11–12; "Le Phénomène spirituel" (1937) in *Oeuvres*, vi (Paris, 1962), pp. 131–139; *Ce que le monde attend en ce moment de l' Eglise de Dieu* (unpublished), 1952, p. 3.

20. S. Kierkegaard, *Fear and Trembling* (Princeton, N.J., Princeton University Press, 1954); D. A. Goulet, "Kierkegaard, Aquinas and the Dilemma of Abraham," *Thought*, 32 (1957), 165–188; R. Jolivet, *Aux sources de l'existentialisme chrétien, Kierkegaard* (Paris, 1958); L. Dupré, *Kierkegaard as Theologian* (New York, Sheed and Ward, 1963). Among the modern Protestants: P. Tillich, *Morality and Beyond* (New York, Harper, 1964); H. Thielicke, *Theologische Ethik* (3 vols., Tübingen, 1951–58); *id., Einführung in die christ-*

liche Ethik (Munich, 1963); D. Bonhoeffer, *Ethik* (Munich, 1963); E. Brunner, *Das Gebot und die Ordnungen. Entwurf einer protestantisch-theologischen Ethik* (Tübingen, 1932); P. Althaus, *Gebot und Gesetz. Zum Thema Gesetz und Evangelium* (Gütersloh, 1952). About all this cf. J. Lhoir, "Le droit naturel chez les théologiens protestants actuels," *Coll. Mechl.*, 1964, pp. 226–252.

21. The only Catholic work which may undoubtedly be labeled as belonging to situation ethics is that of E. Michel, *Ehe. Eine Anthropologie der Geschlechtsgemeinschaft* (Stuttgart, 1948), which was put on the Index because it applied the principles of situation ethics to conjugal morality. Cf. the criticisms of K. Rahner, in "Situationsethik und Sündenmystik," *Stimmen der Zeit*, 145 (1949), 330–342. The main pronouncements of Pius XII can be found in *Acta Apostolicae Sedis* (*AAS*), 42 (1950), 574 (*Humani Generis*); *AAS* 44 (1952), 270–278 (radio message on the Christian conscience); *AAS* 44 (1952), 413–419 (address to the World Federation of Catholic Feminine Youth). The position of the Holy Office, set down on February 2, 1956, has appeared in *AAS* 48 (1956), 144–145.

22. Cf. *AAS* 44 (1952), 415–416.

23. *AAS* 44 (1952), 415.

24. *AAS* 48 (1956), 144–145.

25. Bibliography on situational ethics: J. Fuchs, *Situation und Entscheidung* (Frankfurt, 1952); M. Thurian, *La Confession* (Neuchâtel, 1953); J. Fuchs, "Morale théologique et morale de situation," *Nouv. Rev. Théol.*, 76 (1954), 1073–1085; *id.*, "Ethique objective et éthique de situation," *Nouv. Rev. Théol.*, 78 (1956), 798–818; J. M. Le Blond, "Sincérité et vérité, A propos de la morale de situation," *Etudes*, 292 (1957), 238–256; D. von Hildebrand and Alice Jourdain, *True Morality and Its Counterfeits* (New York, McKay, 1957); R. Gleason, "Situational Morality," *Thought*, 32 (1957), 553–558; P. Tiberghien, "Plaidoyer pour une morale objective," *Mélanges de science religieuse*, 17 (1960), 153–160; W. Schoellgen, *Konkrete Ethik* (Düsseldorf, 1961); J. Daniélou, "La morale au service de la personne," *Etudes*, 317 (1963), 145–153; P. Antoine, "Conscience et loi naturelle," *Etudes*, 317 (1963), 162–183; E. Hamel, *Loi naturelle et loi du Christ* (Bruges, 1964); J. Goffinet, *Morale de situation et morale chrétienne* (Brussels, 1964); P. Delhaye, "Morale ou moralisme," *Suppl. Vie Spir.*, 17 (1964), 243–271; *id.*, "Liberté chrétienne et obligation morale," *Eph. Theol. Lov.*, 40 (1964), 347–

361; D. Dietz, "Conscience and Love: Papal Teaching on Situation Ethics," *Amer. Eccl. Rev.*, 146 (1962), 225–232; W. Wallace, "Existential Ethics (of K. Rahner): A Thomistic Appraisal," *Thomist,* 27 (1963), 493–515.

26. I.IIae, q. 91, a. 2, c. On the theme of this paragraph, see P. Antoine, *op. cit.*

27. P. Teilhard de Chardin, *The Phenomenon of Man,* p. 263. Influenced by Teilhard, J. Onimus, "Métamorphose du mariage?" in *Un livre pour mes filles* (Paris, 1964), pp. 179–198, puts the present crisis of conjugal morality in the perspective of an evolutionary morality.

28. I.IIae, q. 94, a. 4, c.

29. Cf. *S. Theol.*, II.IIae, q. 120, a. 1 and 2. See also R. Egenter, "Ueber die Bedeutung der Epikie im sittlichen Leben," in *Phil. Jahrb.,* 1940, pp. 115–127; B. Häring, "Tugend der Epikie," in *Die gegenwärtige Heilsstunde,* pp. 210–218.

30. G. Soehngen, *Gesetz und Evangelium* (Freiburg, 1957); P. Fransen, *Divine Grace and Man* (New York, Desclée, 1965); J. Potin, "La loi et la liberté selon l'enseignement de Jésus," *Suppl. Vie Spir.*, 17 (1964), 376–390.

31. Cf. T. Deman, *La prudence* (Tournai, 1949); J. Pieper, *Prudence* (New York, Pantheon, 1959).

32. Galatians 3.24–25; see S. Lyonnet, "Saint Paul: Liberty and Law," *The Bridge,* 4 (1961), 229–251. The theme of the law as a pedagogue can already be found in Greek philosophy; see, for instance, Plato, *Laws,* 718 a 15 ff. and 719; Aristotle, *Nicomachean Ethics,* 10.9.

33. Cf. J. M. Le Blond, "Sincérité et vérité," *Etudes,* 292 (1957), 238–256; O. Rabut, *La vérité de l'action* (Paris, 1962).

34. Cf. P. Delhaye, "La théologie morale d'hier et d'aujourd'hui," *Rev. sciences relig.*, 27 (1953), 112–130; L. Beirnaert, "Rôle et attitude du conseiller moral," *Etudes,* 317 (1963), 154–161.

35. Frère Untel, *Les insolences du Frère Untel* (Montreal, 1960), p. 79. See also R. Guardini, *Wille und Wahrheit* (Mainz, 1954), pp. 117–119.

36. Cf. K. Rahner, *Dangers dans le catholicisme d'aujourd'hui* (Paris, 1959), p. 87. See also J. Corbon, *L'expérience chrétienne dans la Bible* (Bruges, 1963), pp. 127–129, and the three principles laid down by Pius XII, in *AAS,* 44 (1952), 417–418.

37. Cf. M. Oraison, *Love or Constraint?* (New York, Kenedy, 1961);

A. Godin, *Le Dieu des parents et le Dieu des enfants* (Tournai, 1963); W. Bitter, *Vorträge über das Vaterproblem* (Stuttgart, 1954); D. Widlocher, "La fonction paternelle," *Etudes*, 316 (1963), 318–329.

38. A. Babin, *Crisis of Faith: the Religious Psychology of Adolescence* (New York, 1963).

39. P. Huizing, "Over kanonieke godsdienstig wetten," in *Nederl. Kathol. Stemmen*, 1962, pp. 323–328.

40. See in Denzinger-Schönmetzer, nos. 3014 and 3036 (in the older editions nos. 1794 and 1815) the condemnation, by Vatican I, of the theory of the equal rights of doubting for believers and unbelievers. For the text of adnotation 20 to the antepreparatory schema of Franzelin, see Mansi, vol. 50, c. 95; a wise commentary of that text in R. Aubert, *Le problème de l'acte de foi* (Louvain, 1945), pp. 200–219, especially this statement: ". . . there is no question at all of an action of grace which would be infallible and clear enough to render any sincere error impossible" (p. 215). See also K. Rahner and H. Vorgrimler, *Kleines theologisches Wörterbuch* (Freiburg, 1961), under "Glaubensabfall" pp. 136–137; M. Steckler, *Instinkt und Glaubenswille nach Thomas von Aquin* (Mainz, 1961), pp. 161–166.

41. F. Dostoyevski, "The Legend of the Grand Inquisitor" in *The Brothers Karamazov*. See also S. Anders, *El Greco malt den Gross-Inquisitor* (Munich, 1955).

42. See K. Rahner, *Die Chancen des Christentums heute* (Cologne, 1952). E. Roche, "Notre conditions de pécheurs," *Nouv. Rev. Théol.*, 72 (1950), 690–703; D. von Hildebrand, *True Morality and Its Counterfeits;* K. Rahner, "Gerecht und Sünder zugleich," *Geist und Leben*, 53 (1963), 434–443.

43. *Op. cit.*, p. 312.

44. S. Kierkegaard, "Three Discourses at the Communion on Fridays," in *Christian Discourses* (New York, Oxford, 1952), p. 371.

45. Matthew 5.20; 15.11–14; 23.13–33, and passim.

46. F. Mauriac, *Thérèse Desqueyroux* (Paris, 1927). The antithesis, "fleeing from God—fleeing towards God" comes from St. Augustine, *Enarrationes in Psalmos*, 74, *P.L.*, 35, col. 953.

Index